THE
COMPLETE
BOOK
OF

# Silk Painting

## DIANE TUCKMAN & JAN JANAS

NORTH LIGHT BOOKS

*Cincinnati, Ohio*

## Here's what they're saying about The Complete Book of Silk Painting . . .

"WOW! is the reaction one has upon opening *The Complete Book of Silk Painting* by Diane Tuckman and Jan Janas."—ARTS & ACTIVITIES

" . . . a 'must' for all surface designers working with dyes, as well as for painters interested in applying their talents to the more sensuous world of the textile arts." — SURFACE DESIGN JOURNAL

"There are no words to describe adequately the art here, you have to see it with your eyes. Even if you never want to paint on silk, this book is worth owning for its artistry."—SEWING & FINE NEEDLEWORK

"The book is packed with experiments that really stretch what you can do with this medium."—FIBERARTS

"Beautiful color photos of steps and designs created by artists from America and Europe show you the versatility of this wonderful art form."—CRAFTWORKS FOR THE HOME

96  95  94  93          5  4  3

**Library of Congress Cataloging in Publication Data**

Tuckman, Diane
      The complete book of silk painting / Diane Tuckman & Jan Janas. — 1st ed.
           p.      cm.
      Includes bibliographical references and index.
      ISBN 0-89134-422-5
      1. Silk painting. 2. Textile painting. I. Janas, Jan. II. Title.
TT851.T83      1992
746.6—dc20                                                     91-31594
                                                                      CIP

Edited by Sheila Freeman
Designed by Paul Neff
Page 121 constitutes an extension of this copyright page.

# ACKNOWLEDGMENTS

We feel that this book has been such a cooperative effort, developed over a period of several years with so many individuals participating in subtle ways, that it would be difficult to remember and pinpoint them all.

We would like to thank directly at least a few people who have been influential. As we mention in the Introduction, Colette Favart-Gouin of Paris, France, constantly and steadfastly encouraged us to write and teach this exciting art form and offered extensive technical advice. We would like to mention Naomi Barsky, artist and silk painter, who helped to bring silk painting into the consciousness of the American art and craft community by teaching and writing on the subject.

We would like to acknowledge the contribution of Bonnie Silverstein who encouraged us to complete the book on time and helped us "beat it into shape!"

Our thanks to Jeff Lapin for his steadfast support, to Lee Stewart and Idaz Greenberg, who graciously reviewed the manuscript to ferret out obvious and not so obvious inconsistencies.

We certainly cannot forget our families, close friends and co-workers who helped with their encouragement and patience. They believed in our dream!

Several of the ideas, suggestions and possibilities included in this book are a direct result of our contacts with individuals in various fields—artists, teachers, students, fiber artists, decorative painters, designers and craftspersons. These bold and adventurous individuals, confronted with the visual impact of silk painting, pursued the art form. To all of those we pay tribute.

# TABLE OF CONTENTS

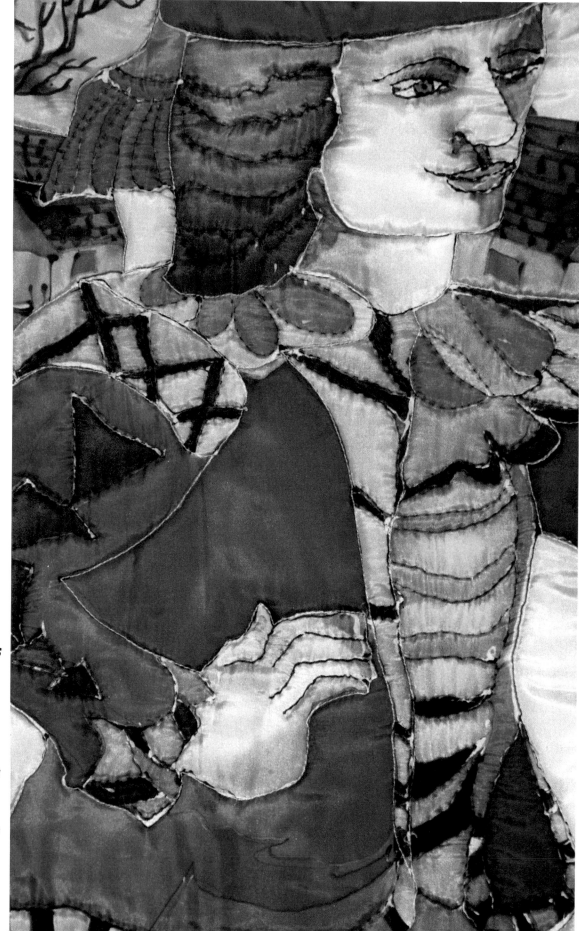

## FARMER BANASZAK AND HIS WIFE, SOPHIE

Jan Janas
Detail of quilted wall hanging
8mm silk, dyes, gutta.

The surface of this painted wall hanging
was enhanced by hand quilting along
all resist lines. The design was
freehanded in resist and then painted in
the watercolor technique. The author
finds the three-dimensional look
effective for wall hangings.

# ABOUT THE AUTHORS

## Diane Tuckman

I was born in Egypt and spent my childhood there. Egypt was an interesting cosmopolitan place to grow up. My parents exposed me to languages, the arts and flowers! In school, there were Friday morning art classes in a large glass-covered room with a garden containing various things to collect, look at, and work with, and that was quite inspiring to me.

After 1948, I lived in Paris, France, for a number of years. It was an exciting time for me, living in a fascinating city that has so much to offer. As a teenager and young adult, I roamed the parks and the historic areas, attended the theatre, and constantly visited the museums.

I met my husband in romantic Paris while he was in the U.S. Military. When his military duty was over, we moved to the United States and settled in Maryland, where we now live. We have two children.

I have always been intrigued by art. When I discovered that information about the French dyes was kept a deep, dark secret by the practitioners of the art form, and that the products were not readily available in the United States, I started my own company, Ivy Imports, in Beltsville, Maryland, to carry a complete line of fabric painting supplies and accessories. I contributed to the popularization of silk painting with what has come to be known as the French dyes, by teaching and writing on the subject so it could be accessible to all. I even coined the expression "silk painting." In France it is known as painting on silk. But I am convinced that we are painting *with* silk and not *on* silk! To that end, I authored the original *Grapevine*, a booklet with hints and information about silk painting. After several updated editions, I co-authored *The Grapevine, a Silk Painting Guide*.

I still run Ivy Imports and frequently conduct workshops in various areas of this country and abroad on the art of silk painting, as well as teaching in videotapes on the art form.

## Jan Janas

Born and raised in Chicago, Illinois, I have pursued my dream of art, studying at Northern Michigan University, the University of Northern Illinois, and the Art Institute of Chicago. I wanted to experience all the art world had to offer, from oil, acrylic and watercolor to ceramics, silversmithing, welding, sculpture, and, finally, fiber art. Upon graduating, I decided to share my knowledge and experience and entered the teaching profession.

In 1989, I published my first work on the subject of fiber painting, titled *Janas' Faces*. Pattern books followed and can be found at arts and crafts shops throughout the United States.

My work has been exhibited in galleries and art museums, and my silk wall hangings and exotic, one-of-a-kind clothing have been purchased extensively for corporate and private collections.

I demonstrate and teach silk and fabric painting across the country. Today, I conduct workshops on the East Coast and travel extensively, demonstrating silk painting for Ivy Imports.

**DIANE TUCKMAN**                    **JAN JANAS**

# INTRODUCTION

## The Silk Route Continues . . .

*"Painted Silks!" For those of us who have a vivid imagination, these words evoke all the mystery and magic of the Orient.*

*Mystery because this precious fabric was the object of a luxury trade by the nomadic caravans that crisscrossed the arid regions of northern China, a then-unknown country at the other end of the world. Along with purple dye, spices, porcelain, glass and paper, silk fabrics were the first products traded between East and West.*

*Magic because of the mysterious origin and cost of this attractive fabric. During the first century before our era, the Romans were the first in the East to admire and use silk. The cost was so great that the Roman Senate had to forbid its import several times.*

*How long and tortuous is the Silk Road, from its genesis in the tight cocoon to its culmination in the painted silk! Venice, Istanbul, Baghdad, Teheran, Samarkand and Tashkent—these places evoke visions of noisy caravans laden with their precious cargoes of fabrics, mingling with the heady perfume of spices and the translucence of glass. In those early days, silk was used as textile for ornamentation and interior decoration, such as wall hangings, cushions and screens. Gradually, silk came into use for wearables. Warm and sumptuous colors were imparted to these coveted fabrics with vegetable dyes such as indigo, madder and saffron.*

*In our time, silk still comes from the Orient in various forms such as fine or heavy, smooth or textured, bright or matte. Sophisticated and indelible liquid colors allow us all to re-create the warm, exotic, distant feel of the East. To that end, this book will open the gates to this multifaceted art form and encourage us to plunge deeply into the delights of silk painting. To us silk painters, the Silk Route remains open.*

*— Colette Favart-Gouin*

## Silk Painting as an Art Form

We would like to thank Mme. Favart-Gouin for contributing the previous essay. Colette is a long-time silk painter but primarily an artist in every sense of the word. She has always worked in many different mediums, and still does. She has contributed to the art of silk painting by teaching the medium to art teachers in France.

Painting with silk is a multifaceted process like the fabric itself. Many strands—or processes—are combined and woven together to produce the *whole cloth*! And when these sumptuous silks are enhanced with exceptionally brilliant liquid colors, which then merge to become an integral part of the fabric, you have an unbeatable combination of art and beauty.

Silk painting is not a static art form. Quite the contrary! Like watercolor, the hallmark of silk painting is its movement and fluidity. But unlike paper, working on silk is truly a sensuous experience. While your hand delicately guides the movement of the liquid colors, they flow and glide through the silk. As you start to paint, you will become one with the process and find a link between the medium and your personal desire to express yourself in an emotional way.

Yes, painting on silk is creating *art* on fabric, with the silk as your canvas. Silk painting can be done on different surfaces, with or without your control, in styles ranging from intricate to free form. The transparency of silk is so exquisite and delicate that you will soon discover colors you never imagined.

**PAINTED SILKS**

*Jan Janas*
*Dyes and paints.*

*Silk offers the fabric artist unlimited possibilities for creative expression when painting with today's sophisticated and indelible liquid colors.*

The formula for enhancing your creativity is simple: EXPRESSION = DISCOVERY. The more you experiment, the more your artistic expression will allow you to stretch your imagination toward ever new horizons. But first you must acquire the skills required by the medium to move toward even more discoveries. And this book will help you to do that.

There is no limit to the search for new ideas. As you discover more and more things to try, you will be fascinated by the subtleties. Never be afraid to make mistakes. What some people may call a mistake, others might consider a happy accident. Mistakes can be your best teacher. Just as in other art forms, silk painting has no do's and don'ts — no absolutes. Avoid preconceptions. Remember, flexibility is a virtue. Just be still and listen to your inner voice.

## Silk Painting as a Craft

Although silk painting is creating art on fabric, some people prefer to regard it as a craft. To that we can only reply: There is nothing wrong with art being functional. Crafts have a long history of excellence as a form of human expression. What can give us greater joy than being surrounded by beautiful objects on a continuous and daily basis, things that become part of our inner subconscious orientation as we move about our environment? Isn't it wonderful to think, "I will see this beautiful silk painting on the wall as I turn the corner"; or "The bedspread will welcome me as I enter the bedroom." When the beautiful things we create and use daily have meaning, purpose, style and are exquisitely executed, seeing them as part of our daily lives is a joyful experience.

## The History of Silk Painting

Historically, fabric painting was very popular in the Far East. How can we forget kimono art in Japan over the centuries? And, of course, remember that silk originated in China. Then there is Indonesia, which gave us batik with all its intricacies, beauty and challenge.

Although the dyes were developed around 1850, it was not until approximately 1920 that silk painting started to develop as we know it today. Russian émigrés fled to Paris and earned a living making exquisite men's silk handkerchiefs. Experimenting, they started to paint on silk fabric and the art of silk painting was born. This soon evolved to painting on other items such as scarves and

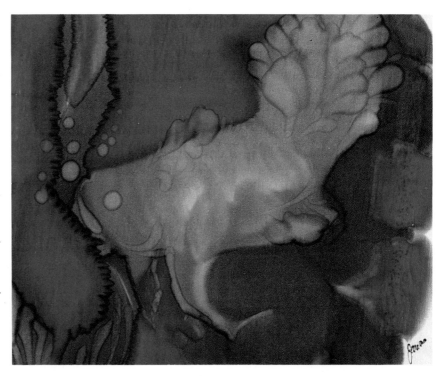

wall hangings and grew to such an extent that at one time there were twenty-six silk painting workshops in Paris.

Artistic expression on fabric has traditionally played a major role in the French fashion industry where fabric designers often use silk painting techniques to animate their ideas for fashion designers. At the end of World War II, with supplies scarce and money tight, designers and the women they designed for looked for ways to express their delight in achieving peace. They turned to decorative scarves to symbolize the times and "le carré"—the square—was born.

With one exquisite square of silk one could show taste, style, color sense and art appreciation. Famous artists were commissioned to design silk squares for reprint, often in limited editions. The House of Ascher, based in London, was particularly successful in having the likes of Henry Moore, Alexander Calder, Henri Matisse and many others design scarves for the fashion industry. Some of you may remember the extensive series of scarves popular in the fifties called "Les Amoureux de Peynet." They are charming lovers depicted with a theme on each scarf. Many an American tourist must have one of those delightful squares in a drawer! And, of course, we cannot fail to mention the famous, chic, Hermes scarves—a must for any woman who can afford one! Interest in scarves as wearable art has never flagged. In fact, these days hand-painted scarves are making a big resurgence

**GOLD FISH**

*12″ × 12″*

*Jan Janas*

*8mm silk, dyes, alcohol.*

*The wet-on-wet technique was used in this painting to capture the depth and fluidity of water. The alcohol solution was used after the dyes had dried to brush in air bubbles and details.*

because the popularity of silk painting allows everyone to create their own "carré."

In 1965, Litza Bain, a Parisian artist, came across some of the techniques of silk painting first used by the Russian émigrés to France, and those of the milliners and silk flower makers. Researching their techniques, she combined all these elements (or strands!) into a system for painting on silk as an art form and started to teach it, finding group teaching a wonderful way to share her enthusiasm for her discoveries. She also encouraged French art supply manufacturers to create the products she needed. Her clear, detailed records and photographs of the processes of painting on silk, coupled with her enthusiastic "why not try this" attitude soon created a good-sized following of students and colleagues who wanted to paint on silk—and silk painting became open to everyone to try and enjoy!

## About This Book

There are many ways to paint on fabric, and many types of fabrics to do it on, but the focus of this book is on authentic silk painting. This means we will be using the traditional silk painting dyes—known as French dyes—that work on silk and wool only and require steam setting. Some artists

**KIMONO**
Jan Janas
Silk broadcloth, dyes, gold and black paint resist.

"My design is very involved with symbols and stylized faces of oriental influence," says Janas. "I used the gold and black resist not only to restrict the movement of the dyes but also to embellish the surface of the fabric."

**IMPRESSION OF A BUTTERFLY**
19" × 26"  Joan Griffin
Douppioni silk, French dyes, wax resist, alcohol.

In this painting, the artist created an exciting abstract of movement and texture through the repeated use of lines and dots. A wax resist was used for containment of dyes in the large shapes.

have found that these dyes also work on rayon, nylon, feathers and leather. Please experiment first. The newer liquid resin-based paints work on all fabrics and can be set with an iron. You will find that the techniques in this book are applicable to both.

To begin, we recommend that you first learn the silk painting vocabulary. Become familiar with the tools; understand how the process works before learning specific techniques. We have organized the book following this idea. Each chapter is self-contained and organized in a logical progression of detailed information. You will find important facts in this book and some less critical hints.

## Who Will Enjoy Silk Painting?

There is something in silk painting for everyone, no matter what your level of expertise. Children enjoy its immediacy and easy application. Art teachers and students are aware of its potential. Quilters use the lines of resist as quilting lines, and weavers paint intricate shadow designs on their warps. Fashion designers and interior decorators use silk painted fabrics for clothing and the home. Professionals appreciate the intricacies and sophistication of the medium, and artists and craftspersons are attracted by its challenge.

This book is divided into four sections. The first is on the materials and supplies needed for silk painting—the fabrics, resists, brushes and dyes required. We will also suggest ways to set up your work area.

The second section takes you through the basics of how to use the materials described in Section One. These are the procedures required to create a silk painting, from selecting a design to stretching the fabric onto a frame, to applying the colors, then setting the dyes.

The third section deals with specific techniques for applying the dyes to get unusual and interesting effects. Here you will learn about resists, blending and double loading the brush, using salt and alcohol for special effects, working wet-on-wet, dry-brush and many, many more techniques.

Finally we have ended this book on a high note by inviting some talented silk painters to share their work and ideas about silk painting. This is an "idea" section as well as a gallery, and hopefully should entice you to try new ways of using this fascinating painting medium to create beautiful objects.

**SCARF AND EARRINGS**

Sharon Adee

19mm silk Charmeuse, French dyes, wax batik.

Notice the strong design, the application of layered, jewel-toned colors and the beautiful drape and hand of the heavy Charmeuse fabric. The dyes are simply painted on.

## *Experiment to Learn*

In this book, we would like to stress two things: (1) TEST, TEST, TEST, and (2) PRACTICE, PRACTICE, PRACTICE! Purchase some silk by the yard in different weights and consider that your learning investment. Classes are a good way to learn quickly in a concentrated setting. This, however, does not take the place of experimentation.

We have written this book to provide you with enough technical information and knowledge to master the basics. But we don't want you to get so lost in the technical material that you forget to enjoy yourself. We also want you to use this information to get new ideas, to experiment and create your own style of silk painting. Finally, we hope that despite the abundant amount of information in this book, our enthusiasm for silk painting shows through, because, above all, silk painting is fun! Consider this an open invitation to join us and share our passion for silk painting!

At the time this book is being published, several individuals are trying to establish a silk painting network to exchange ideas. (If you wish to be part of such a network, you can add your name to our list of "silk painting friends" by writing us ℅ North Light Books, 1507 Dana Avenue, Cincinnati, Ohio 45207.) We hope this idea will come to fruition as the Silk Route continues to stretch ever outward and onward. . . .

— *Diane Tuckman & Jan Janas*

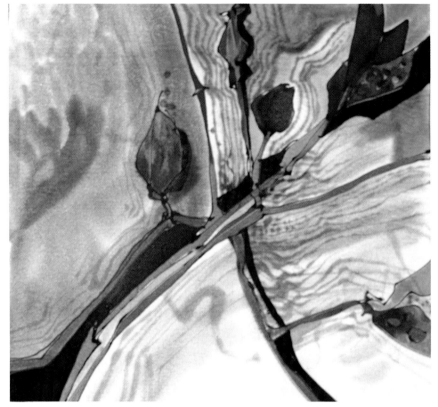

**BRANCH**

*12″ × 12″ Jan Janas*
*8mm silk, dyes, resist.*

*A few quick resisted lines suggested a branch on a budding tree. Light washes and lines of color were applied to create the movement of the wind.*

**THE PLAY GARDEN**

*(Detail)*
*36″ × 36″ Jan Janas*
*5mm silk, dye, wax resist.*

*"Most of my silk paintings are visual dialogues I make up as I freehand my design in resist on the silk," says Janas. "The designs are spontaneous and usually quite intricate. I do not worry about mistakes. In fact, the happy accidents that occur are a challenge for me to integrate into my design. I sharpen my painting and drawing skills this way."*

# 1 *Knowing Your Materials*

Before we discuss the process of silk painting, you will need to become familiar with the materials involved. Some of this information will be repeated later when we discuss the procedures and individual techniques; this is unavoidable. But we intend this section to serve as an introduction to the terminology used in silk painting as well as to describe the basic and essential ingredients of this artistic medium.

In this section you will learn about the work space and how to set it up, you'll get a checklist of materials you will need, and we will discuss some of the more important basic materials (fabrics, resists, dyes and applicators or brushes) at some length. This section will also serve as a handy reference later when you start to paint. So take the time to review it much as you would read a recipe before baking or cooking.

As with any hobby or interest, finding an adequate, comfortable and efficient work space is a challenge! You need to consider storage space as well. Here are a few suggestions.

## Work Area

If you're trying to find work space in your home, consider an area away from the center of daily activities—one that won't require constant clean-up every time you stop painting. Then plan your environment, working surfaces, equipment location and storage space. Remember, organization is the key!

Just as the size of the frame you'll be stretching your fabric on determines the space you need, the size of the work area you have available may influence the size of your work. The larger the project, the more space you'll need. Try to leave enough room to walk around the frame allowing you to view and reach your work from all directions. For small items, you can work on a table, turning the frame around as needed.

To save steps and time, it's convenient to have an electrical outlet to plug in a steamer, iron or hair dryer. A sink close by is also handy.

It is preferable to work on a white surface. The white background will help you transfer the design easily and won't affect your perception of the colors. If the combination of white silk, white background and bright light gives off too much glare, use a black background to apply the resist (see chapter 4), then change back to the white background. Remember to protect your floor with plastic because these products will permanently stain some surfaces. If you spill anything, remove it immediately. Traditional silk painting dyes will come off with alcohol or a water/alcohol solution, and repeated applications help. Bleach-based cleaning products, detergents and soaps are also sometimes effective with resin-based products.

**TABORET.** A small rolling cart with shelves is also very practical. Before you start a project, particularly a large one, place all the items you will need on the cart: the selected colors, resists in the applicators, brushes, paper towels, water/alcohol solution or diluent (more commonly known as "dilutant"), pins, alcohol, cotton swabs, extra mixing cups, and two containers with clean water. Attach a strip of fabric to the side of the cart to allow you to sample the colors as you work. You can move the cart around the frame. It helps minimize the chance of spilling because you will have a convenient surface close by, and if you start painting and decide to make a quick change, everything will be at your fingertips.

*This nine-foot table was built for Janas's studio. It's wonderful to work on. The plywood top panels can be removed easily to convert it into a nine-foot stretcher for silk painting.*

**WORKTABLE.** If you are working with a relatively small project, all you need is a table that will accommodate the size of your frame and space to put the supplies you are using. Try to set it up properly. If the frame is not at the proper height you may get backaches and find standing very tiring.

When working on a small project, if the fabric sags, raise the frame on blocks if you cannot restretch the fabric. You can also adjust the height of the table by using bricks or cinder blocks and sitting on an adjustable stool. Some silk painters who work on large surfaces for long periods of time sit on a typing chair with wheels and roll it along, particularly when applying intricate resist onto a large project.

**LIGHTING.** Because you're constantly dealing with color, color perception and silk, good lighting is essential. Silk is shiny and sometimes creates a glare. If the lighting is not good, your colors will be distorted. Since color plays such an important role, it must be accurate. So, if you are currently using fluorescent lighting, daylight bulbs are a good investment. Good lighting is also important when using resists because it is sometimes difficult to see them on white fabric.

**WEATHER CONDITIONS.** Excessive heat and drafts will dry dyes and paints too quickly. This will make using salt and blending large surfaces difficult. Hot, dry conditions also promote the quick formation of dark edge lines, rings and halos (sometimes called aureolas). Avoid heavy air movement from fans, open windows and air-conditioning, which dries the air and promotes undesirable accelerated drying.

Too much dampness and humidity, on the other hand, may force you to wait longer than usual for the resists to dry before you start to paint. But when your colors dry slower in the humidity, you'll have more time to blend and avoid the formation of the dark edge line. Salt, which can be sprinkled on dyes and paints to produce beautiful effects (see chapter 15), works best when the humidity is lower.

**VENTILATION.** Like other art materials, the pigments you'll use for silk painting require good ventilation. Most authentic silk painting dyes contain alcohol, and if you paint for long periods of time, you need to eliminate the fumes. Keep your bottles capped—alcohol fumes dissipate slowly. The dyes are nontoxic, but you'll need to aerate the area. Use

*A silk painting can be done with cotton swabs, which keep the artist's painting style loose and facilitate quick color changes. The egg carton keeps the small paint-filled plastic cups from tipping over.*

an exhaust fan; opening windows and arranging for cross ventilation helps. If you're sensitive to alcohol, there are traditional silk painting dyes on the market that don't contain alcohol. The gutta resists contain petroleum distillates, and the vapors from these products require elimination. Furthermore, the guttas and the solvents are flammable, so keep them away from open flames.

In short, keep a commonsense approach. If you are especially sensitive, you may wish to wear a vapor mask. But for most people, a large, well-ventilated area is sufficient, and even though the dyes are nontoxic, keep them out of the reach of children, like any art product.

**ADDITIONAL HINTS.** Plan a well-organized storage area and you won't regret it, particularly when you're painting and rushing to find something.

Store the silk painting dyes and the resists in a cool, dark place. Don't expose the products to extreme heat or freezing cold, and for best results, keep the gutta and water-soluble resists in the refrigerator. Store all mixed colors you've finished working with in plastic bottles, one for each color family (e.g., one for all the reds, one for the blues, and so forth). Leftovers that don't fit any general container can be placed into an odds and ends bottle (excellent for backgrounds). All colors you put away for future use should be labeled as to content and color mixture because it's difficult to tell what is in old containers.

You can store various items in plastic boxes so you can see them quickly. A pegboard with hooks is also handy for storing frames, assembled and unassembled, as well as all other kinds of supplies such as scissors and strips of fabric.

*A rolling supply cart is great to have when you are working on a large silk painting. You just move the cart around the frame as you work.*

Silk painting also requires a certain amount of concentration, so try to work in a quiet atmosphere, free of interruptions. You will get very engrossed in your painting and interruptions will tend to distract you. Take the phone off the hook when applying resist or painting large areas so you don't have to decide to answer it or not.

As a general rule, it's best not to work outdoors when doing silk painting, though some artists working with the free techniques prefer doing just that.

The temperature affects the resists and they will become completely ineffective in the heat and sun. Also, painted colors dry too quickly in moving air, flying particles or insects can land on your fabric, and sudden rain can easily hit your fabric and mar your work.

Now that you are set up, put on old clothes, comfortable shoes and music. You are ready to relax and enjoy silk painting!

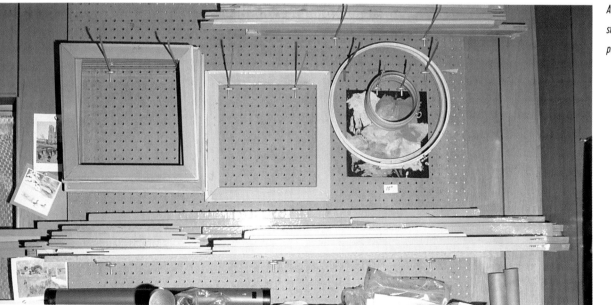

*A pegboard with hooks is handy for storing frames as well as other silk painting supplies.*

# MATERIALS AND SUPPLIES

The following checklist will help you purchase and assemble the supplies needed for silk painting. Several items are marked optional because they are only necessary for very specific silk painting techniques. Purchase what you need as you go along.

***Dyes and paints.*** The following materials are available at art supply stores, craft shops and fabric stores (request them if they do not carry them): Traditional silk painting dyes for silk and wool, available in a variety of colors and concentrations; resin-based fabric paints for all types of fabrics, available in a wide variety of colors.

***Fabrics.*** The following supplies are available from specialty fabric painting suppliers and some fabric stores: Silk and wool for authentic silk painting. These fabrics should be Prepared For Printing (PFP), or you must prewash them. All fabrics can be used for resin-based paints. In addition to silk and wool, you can use cotton, rayon, synthetics, linen, blends and other fabrics. Avoid fabrics with a finish, particularly permanent press.

***Frames for stretching fabric.*** Canvas stretcher strips (available from art supply stores and craft shops); adjustable frames, made from lumber and C-clamps (available at hardware stores); embroidery hoops (optional—at craft shops and knitting stores).

***Pins.*** Stainless steel pushpins; three-prong pins (optional); extra long pins (optional).

***Resists to define and control colors.*** Gutta serti; Gutta solvent; water-based resist; wax (optional).

***Resist applicators.*** Squeeze bottles with spout; metal tips with pins; paper cones (optional); stiff brushes (optional); tjantings (optional wax applicator).

***Containers.*** Lidded jars or plastic bottles; water containers; welled palettes; small, lidded plastic cups; clear cups or jars.

***Diluents.*** Prepared concentrates for traditional silk painting dyes; water/alcohol solution (ethyl rubbing alcohol); concentrated diluent for resin-based paints. (Also spelled *dilutant.*)

***Salt.*** Table salt; sea salt; kosher salt; rock salt.

***Alcohol.*** Ethyl rubbing alcohol 70 percent (available at drug stores).

***Thickeners.*** Silk screen thickener for traditional silk painting dyes; thickening gel for resin-based paints; antifusants.

***Design supplies.*** Pictures, books, photos, etc; tracing paper; newsprint for drawing sketches; waterproof felt-tip pens; ruler, pencils, tape; tracing pens, all-surface pens, fine charcoal.

***Brushes.*** Natural-hair brushes, watercolor-type; assorted brushes—fan, bristle, scrubbers, synthetic (optional); foam brushes; foam applicators.

***Fabric pens.*** Indelible fabric pens for detail and signing.

***Supplies for setting fabrics.*** For steam setting silk painting dyes: large lidded pot with rack; newsprint or fabric sheeting; aluminum foil. For setting resin-based paints: iron and ironing board; press cloth; fixative (if required).

***Miscellaneous supplies.*** Distilled water; paper towels (very absorbent); rags; droppers; stirrers; white vinegar; atomizer and spritzer bottles; hair dryer; sharp scissors; packing tape; egg carton; cotton swabs; paper pad for notes.

***Precautions.*** Some silk painting materials are flammable. Work away from all open flames and avoid inhaling the fumes. Work in a well-ventilated area and keep your bottles capped when not in use. Like all art products, these materials should be kept out of the reach of children.

*Sometimes the strangest "found objects" can be useful for resist applicators or will produce unusual textures in silk painting: toothbrush for splattering, sponge for stamping, corrugated cardboard for rubbings, or foam packing shapes for a stencil in misting!*

To work well with your fabrics, you must know something about them, how they work with the dyes, and how to care for them. In this chapter, we will learn about silk, wool and other fabrics you may be working with. Of course, the basis for silk painting is SILK, and we shall dwell on this wonderful fabric at length.

## Working with Silk

Once considered an exotic and expensive fabric only for the rich, silk is now accessible to everyone. Because of its appeal, production has increased dramatically and it is more readily available at reasonable cost.

A fabric used for clothes or home furnishings must be beautiful, comfortable, drape well and take color easily. Silk fulfills all these requirements plus many more. It is lightweight, absorbs moisture, and regains its shape easily. It is also very strong and durable. It can be washed, dry-cleaned, and is easy to maintain. Silk adds romance to wearable art and drama to any room because of its various textures, colors and softness.

Wearing silk is an elegant and sensuous experience. Silk, considered the "Queen of Fabrics," has held a fascination for centuries, in fact 4,000 years, since it was first produced in China. Silk garments can look casual or dressy and elegant. The brightness and iridescence produced by the colors give silk painted fabrics a unique fresh, clear look.

Traditional silk painting dyes have an affinity for animal fibers. (Silk comes from the silkworm and wool from sheep.) You may find that these dyes work for you on other fabrics such as nylon and rayon. You must learn about the fabrics you use in silk painting so you can knowledgeably select the correct fabric for a particular use. We will first talk about silk and then about wool.

**MAIN CHARACTERISTICS.** Silk is an animal fiber made of protein in a continuous filament. The thread of the silkworm is very fine but resilient. A cocoon can give you a thread that is one kilometer long! Silk is highly resilient, so garments made of silk keep their shape. The sericin in the silk allows it to retain a vast quantity of water, and that makes the fabric very comfortable to wear. The weight, width and length are used to determine the *momme* ("weight") of a particular fabric. Momme is a Japanese unit of weight used in silk production. One momme is .13228 of one ounce. There are 120.96 momme to a pound of silk. For example: a square yard of 8 momme China silk (abbreviated 8mm) weighs one ounce. In essence, the heavier the fabric, the higher the momme number.

Silk is available in a wide variety of textures and qualities. Irregularities in the weave are in the nature of silk, and part of its charm and appeal, and are not to be considered flaws. With experience, you will be able to determine the quality of silk. Quality silk should have body and feel good to the touch (commonly expressed as "having a good hand" or feel).

**TESTING FOR SILK: THE BURN TEST.** Silks used for silk painting must be 100 percent silk or a mixture of silk and wool, but fabrics are not always labeled correctly. If you are not sure your fabric is 100 percent silk, you can do a burn test which will, by the characteristics of odor, combustion and residue, reveal what type of fabric it is. Pull some fibers from the fabric—be sure you include some fibers from the warp (length) and the weft (width)—and roll them into a strand. Then ignite them in a glass dish.

Animal fibers burn slowly and have a distinct odor. Wool smells like hair or chicken feathers and will leave a black, hollow, irregular bead which crumbles easily into a gritty powder. Silk has a milder odor than wool and may smell more like charred or burning meat. It has no sulphur content

**5MM CHINA SILK**

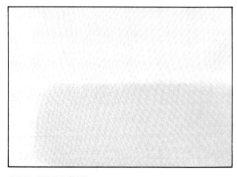

**8MM CHINA SILK**

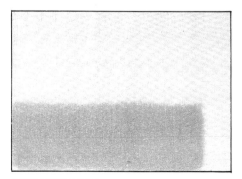

**10MM CHINA SILK**

like wool. Vegetable fibers such as cotton and linen, on the other hand, will burn quickly, with an active flame. Burning flax, hemp, jute, ramie and rayon have the same characteristics as cotton. The odor will be of paper burning, leaving a residue of ashes.

**COLOR AND SILK.** Traditional silk painting dyes are transparent, and they do not contain white. When you need white, simply do not paint that area. White or off-white silk combines well with the beautiful silk painting dyes. Painting on colored silks will be discussed later in Part Three.

For best results, select silk that has been Prepared For Printing (PFP), which means that the fabric has been degummed and has no finish. Always use the best quality silk you can buy because cheap silk is not worth your time and effort. Buy your silk from reliable sources. Poor-quality silk will cause problems because it is weighted with chemicals and sometimes has spots. If the fabric has been permanently pressed or sueded, the dyes will not penetrate the fabric.

**CHOOSING A SILK FOR PAINTING.** There are many types of silk available, with many different weights, weaves and textures, each with its own unique look and feel. When selecting silk for painting, keep in mind the end use of the fabric and whether wearability is a factor. Different types of silks will also react differently to the dyes.

Consider their characteristics before making a choice. Is the fabric smooth or textured, heavy or lightweight? Is it shiny or dull? These characteristics will affect the way the dyes take to the fabric and the final effects will be quite different. For example, you can make a pillow out of any silk—8mm China silk, tussah, twill, crepe de Chine, shantung, noil, Charmeuse or anything in between—and in each case the look will be different.

## Types of Silks: Their Qualities and Use

It is impossible to list all the silks available because of changes in fashion and commercial improvements in the industry. For instance, ribbon silk (striped satin and chiffon) was suddenly available with gold and silver threads woven in. Then it disappeared for a while, and now it is starting to come back.

Silk comes in various weights (5mm, 8mm, 10mm and higher) and in different weaves and looks (twill, crepe de chine, broadcloth, douppioni, noil, honan, tussah, shantung, taffeta, charmeuse, satin, chiffon). Specialty silks may combine two or more of the above types.

**CHINA SILK** (sometimes called *habutai* or *paj*) is an all-purpose silk and the most common type used for silk painting. It has an even weave and a smooth surface, so the resists penetrate easily, and dyes flow quickly and evenly. China silk is available in 5mm, 8mm, 10mm and higher weights. The heavier the silk, the stiffer it is, and the slower the colors flow.

China silk has a nice sparkle and is economical and easy to work with, although the heavier weights do not drape very well. The 5mm weight is good to learn on. Among other uses, it works well for linings, kites and lightweight scarves for a gossamer look. It is recommended that you dilute the dyes because lighter weight fabrics can retain only a certain amount of dye.

The 8mm weight is average and is used for scarves, ties, curtains, lamp shades, pillows and some clothing such as a vest that will be lined. Heavier weights are shinier, with more sparkle and the colors appear deeper. They are used for pillows, wall hangings, framed art and items that require more body.

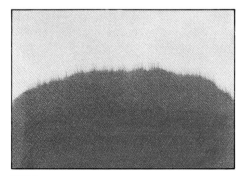

**TWILL**

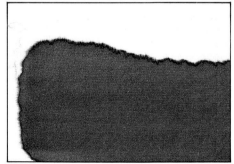

**CREPE DE CHINE**

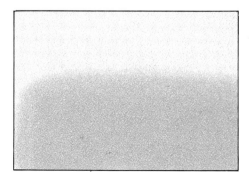

**16MM HEAVY CREPE**

**TWILL SILK** is considered the queen of silk painting because it gives a rich look! It is available in various weights such as 10mm, 12mm, and 14mm but is usually found in 14mm. It has a nice sheen but does not sparkle too much. Because of its diagonal weave, you must apply the resists carefully and use heavier lines, since the diagonal threads can carry the colors in a specific direction.

The dyes come out warm and deep on twill silk and the colors move easily on the fabric, yet with a certain amount of body. Numerous techniques are effective and the fabric drapes well. Use it for pillows, ties, yardage, garments, quilting, wall hangings and long shawls.

**CREPE DE CHINE** is a different type of silk. It does not have too much sheen but it drapes beautifully and has a velvety feel. It is available in 14mm or 16mm and lighter weights. It is excellent for clothing and shawls, but we prefer not to use it for wall hangings, because it easily becomes distorted. It has a textured surface and when you paint on it, the colors flow unevenly. You need to "work" it. It is more difficult to paint even backgrounds with this fabric, and it is hard to put resist lines on it; yet good resist lines are a must. A shiny lightweight crepe (called "flat crepe") is newly available that is truly spectacular. It paints and drapes very well and has a good feel to it.

**BROADCLOTH** is a silk with nice body and weight with low luster, which is good for garments and certain styles of wall hangings. It has an even tight weave, rugged surface and is usually available in natural color. Dyes take well to it. Because of its tight weave and weight, broadcloth works very well without resist. The edges of the painted areas are slightly feathered but not objectionable. Lined with a 5mm or 8mm China silk, broadcloth makes a truly elegant suit or coat and is perfect for wall hangings, especially ones with abstract designs.

**DOUPPIONI** is similar to silk broadcloth and linen, but the surface is harsher and has slubs, which makes the dyes flow less evenly. It is sturdy, yet flexible, which makes it a favorite of many designers. It is also good for tailored garments and wall hangings.

**PONGEE** is made from the silk of uncultivated silkworms. It is somewhat similar to douppioni with slubs and nubs but because it is smoother, silk pongee is easier to paint on, takes colors well, and reflects them effectively. It is usually ecru or natural in color, has a nice hand and is good for home decor items.

**NOIL** is made from waste silk left over after the better silks are made, which is why its threads are short and tightly twisted, giving it a nubby surface. Sometimes called raw silk, noil has the appearance of cotton and is quite economical. There are several varieties of noil. Noil comes bleached or natural with low luster — but if it lacks life, the noil is of poor quality. Noil drapes well but it also clings, so it is best suited to flowing and casual garments and items for home decor.

Foam brushes work well for painting on noil. When you outline the shape you want, the color remains stable and you get a light halo around the colors. If you want a sharper, cleaner look, use a pen to define the lines.

**TUSSAH** is a popular Indian silk, very uneven in weave, heavy and dull but with an interesting texture. It is sometimes called wild silk because, like pongee, it is the product of uncultivated silkworms. It is available in bleached as well as natural color in different degrees of beige. It always has some darker threads running through it, and they cause the dyes to take unevenly, creating unique, interesting highs and lows. Colors usually come out duller on tussah, with a faded look that is very interesting, but bright, bold colors are spectacular.

Because the uneven threads don't allow resists to penetrate well, they are difficult to use. So if you use a resist, be sure the lines are very wide and paint quickly before they become invisible.

Tussah is good for decorative items for the home such as large casual pillows, easy garments or simply tailored clothes.

**SHANTUNG** is similar to tussah, but is more refined. The texture is not as rough, but the strong horizontal slubs are there. It has a shiny surface and that makes it harder for the dyes to penetrate. Using the resist technique is not advisable because the dyes do not flow. On the other hand, working wet-on-wet produces good results. Shantung is available in several weights and is often used in the fashion industry for tailored suits and outfits. It has body and drapes better after being washed. It looks best when painted with subtle colors.

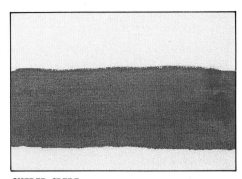

**SUEDED CREPE**

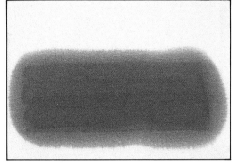

**BROADCLOTH**

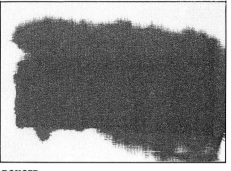

**PONGEE**

**NOIL**

**SHANTUNG**

**CHARMEUSE**

**TAFFETA** is nice to paint on. It feels like the 10mm or heavier china silks. Because it has a slightly rougher surface and is stiffer than the other silks, you will need to adjust to this surface when you paint. Taffeta is used for showy garments that require a stiffer look.

**CHARMEUSE** is the most sensuous of the silks we have discussed so far. Charmeuse comes in a variety of weights, qualities and types. We're giving only general information here. It is usually very heavy and shiny on the right side and dull on the wrong side and is sometimes crepe-backed. Charmeuse drapes and hangs well. It also takes well to dyes, and the colors come out looking brilliant. Both subtle and bold colors are effective.

Resist works well on Charmeuse as long as the lines are broad enough to penetrate the fabric adequately. You must paint on it quickly, unless you paint wet-on-wet, because it has a tendency to form dark edge lines rapidly.

Charmeuse is excellent for intimate garments, blouses and exotic outfits, and for the large dramatic wall hangings you dream of!

**SATIN** is similar to Charmeuse and is, in fact, often mistaken for it. However, it is usually not backed and does not have the same body as Charmeuse.

Shiny and beautiful on the right face, satin silk can be used for the same purposes as Charmeuse, although it is sometimes slightly stiffer.

**SHEER SILKS** such as chiffon and crepe georgette have the same general characteristics as the other silks, but are transparent and lightweight, fall very nicely, and are great for fashionable, dramatic effects when used as overgarments. Because of their texture and weight, they dry very quickly.

Dark edge lines form swiftly on these sheer fabrics, which means you can paint without resist, which is great fun and will give you exquisite results.

Long, flowing designs work best. For example, wet the chiffon with water, paint flowers with a large brush. After the chiffon dries, go back with darker colors around the flowers for contrast.

Also try juxtaposing one color against another on the dry fabric. These fabrics are magnificent for transparent overlays of sheer fabric over heavier fabric.

**ORGANZA** is stiff and transparent. It is difficult to paint on and has limited use for the purposes of this book. However, it is good for smaller items and linings. Organza is also excellent for overlays.

**KNITS** are a completely different type of surface to

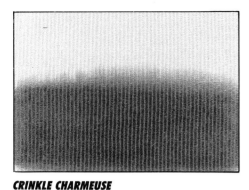

**CRINKLE CHARMEUSE**

**SATIN**

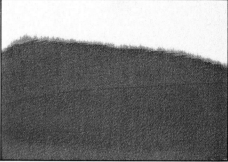

**CHIFFON**

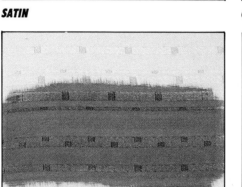

**RIBBON SATIN GEORGETTE**

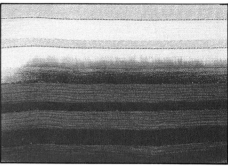

**RIBBON SATIN CHIFFON**

**JACQUARD**

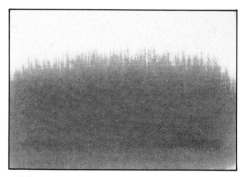

**WOOL**

paint and you will have to experiment with them, since much depends on the tightness of the weave and the weight of the fabric.

*JACQUARD* silk has a design woven into it, white on white. Since the design is in a shinier relief, the light picks up and reflects the highlights in the design and it appears to shimmer. When dyes are applied to it, the raised design gives a lovely dimension to the fabric. Jacquard is fun to paint on. The designs can be enhanced, followed, or ignored. It's especially good for wearable art because the shiny areas really pick up the colors and the effect is dramatic.

*OTHER SILKS.* You will sometimes come across silks that are not as readily available: peau de soie, batiste, bourrette, brocade, crepe georgette, faille and

fugi, to name a few. Then there is "wrinkled silk," which is great for our fast-paced times. Wrinkled silk can easily be machine washed and dried. Its slightly wrinkled look is very fashionable, and it helps overcome the attitude most people have about silk and how difficult it is to care for. You can either purchase it prewrinkled or you can wrinkle it yourself.

Here is how you prewrinkle silk: Use 8mm China silk and wash it gently in the washing machine with a very small amount of soap. Place it in the dryer and use the gentle cycle. The fabric will then be ready to paint and need not be ironed in the future.

## Preparing Silk for Painting

To start, use 5mm or 8mm China silk or experiment with other fabrics. If you feel it is necessary, simply prewash the fabric by hand in cool water with a very mild soap such as baby shampoo or castile soap. Rinse well and put white vinegar in the final rinse, about one tablespoon per bucket. Roll up in a towel and squeeze (do not wring!) and iron while still damp. You are now ready to paint on it.

Pre-hemmed scarves that have rolled edges are a blessing to silk painters who don't sew! They give you a quick visual idea of the project. They are available in a wide variety of sizes, weights and weaves. The most popular is the 8mm China silk.

Overall, when it comes to fabrics for silk painting, you will find that experimenting will be very rewarding. It will give you a feel for the fabrics you prefer to paint with and the wide range of possibilities and limitations.

## Caring for Silk

Very thin silks don't wear as well as the heavier ones because the threads separate and the fabric looks weak and worn. So handle lightweight silks more carefully than the others. Don't bleach silk. Like other fabrics, silk does not take too kindly to being exposed to sunlight.

It is best to place silk garments on padded hangers on a regular basis. When traveling, wrap your silks in tissue paper and steam in between wearings if they become wrinkled. Perspiration is the enemy of silk, so wash your silks often. Washing actually revitalizes silk. Most silks drape better and have a softer hand after the first washing.

**WASHING INSTRUCTIONS.** We highly recommend washing silks. Washing, in fact, is good for the silk—it restores some of the luster and gives it bounce. "Dry Clean Only" labels are found on garments for the protection of the retailers. Individuals who damage their silks through machine washing may attempt to return them as defective merchandise. We have had luck hand-washing almost all types of silk. Only garments having complicated construction with lots of seams, and heavy silks such as "palace silks" and brocades, should not be washed. And when it comes to yardage and very heavy fabrics, dry cleaning is also recommended. Treat your silks as you would your own hair because silk is a protein (animal) fiber.

***Prewashing.*** Sizing and finish are usually added to improve the body of fabric. Some sizings tend to repel paints and dyes. Fabrics that are Prepared For Printing (PFP) usually do not require washing. Always test the silk by washing a small piece first. If the colors don't flow, there is a finish on it. Unless you are sure the silk you purchased is of good quality, it is safer to prewash it. Even reliable suppliers do not have complete control over the goods they purchase. Fabrics that will be used for garments should be prewashed so any shrinkage will take place before the garment is sewn. This is especially critical with wool and crepe de Chine, which will shrink. It is recommended that at-home sewers pretreat their fabrics the same way that they plan to treat them after their garments are sewn. If you expect to dry-clean fabric, do so before painting; if you plan to wash the fabric, do it first.

To prewash your unpainted silks, gently hand wash them in lukewarm water and a mild, neutral soap such as Ivory, baby shampoo or castile soap. Don't use detergents. Soak the silk for a couple of minutes and agitate it gently. Rinse it well in lukewarm water. Add a small amount of white vinegar to the final rinse. Vinegar sometimes helps set the colors after painting and steam setting. It adds bounce to the silk because the sericin (protective silk gum) is restored and the soap residue removed. A small amount of vinegar can also be used to brighten yellowed silk.

To remove the excess moisture from the silk after washing, roll it up in a terry towel and squeeze gently until damp dry or hang it. Do *not* wring the fabric. When washing a silk garment, place it on a padded hanger after removing the excess moisture and keep both sides of the garment separated because sometimes the color will transfer from one to the other.

When the silk is partially dry but still damp, use a dry iron to press the fabric on the back, using the wool setting. If you decide to dry-clean it, you can use a bulk dry-cleaning facility if you have one in your area. It is fast and more economical. Your silks and wool will require very little ironing with this method of cleaning.

## Cutting Silk Fabrics

Always use good, sharp scissors to cut silk. Snip the fabric about a half an inch at the selvage (edge of fabric) and using both hands, rip "smartly"—with a sharp ripping action—across the goods from selvage to selvage. When you reach the other selvage, use the scissors again to cut that selvage. Some silks can also be ripped in the other direction, parallel to the warp. If the silk cannot be ripped, place it on a table covered with another fabric so the silk will not move. Use a yardstick and mark off the length with a pencil at intervals and then cut with the scissors along the markings. Several types of fabrics cannot be ripped and must be cut by this method in both directions.

## Working with Wool

Wool is the other major fabric preferred for use with traditional silk painting dyes. It is a very exciting fabric to use but very different from silk. Because it is heavier, wool takes color differently, with unusual results. Choose lightweight wools that are preferably PFP. Heavy wools are more difficult to paint.

Don't scrub the wool when you paint because it will bring up the nap. Due to the nature of wool, it will absorb a large amount of dye, so dilute your dyes or they will be too intense. Prepare the diluting solution (50 percent water and 50 percent alcohol), then add some alcohol for better penetration and to improve the flow (about a teaspoon of alcohol to one cup of dye).

When working with wool, the lines of resist need to be wide to be effective. It is also a good idea to gray the resist when working on wool so you can see it better (normally it quickly disappears into the nap). You can accomplish that by adding a small amount of black gutta to the clear gutta. Be aware that the colors spread and dry very slowly. Free-flowing techniques are very effective because the colors continue to move on the fabric to create very unexpected and unusual effects. Painted wool is good for framed art because of the lushness of the colors, and it works well for garments, particularly shawls and capes. After you wear wool, allow it to breathe and rest by placing the garment on a padded hanger that fits to avoid distortion.

Silk/wool combinations are also wonderful to paint. These fabrics are very luxurious and easy to work with. They are not easy to find but, when you do, give them a try.

As for care, lightweight wool can be hand washed or dry-cleaned.

To cut wool in a straight line it can be ripped if it is woven loosely, or you can sometimes pull out a thread and use that line to cut a perfect line across the fabric (this is also possible on heavy silks). Keep the fabric as straight as possible to avoid distortion.

## Fabrics for Resin-Based Paints

All types of fabrics can be painted with resin-based paints including, of course, silk and wool. Some fabrics will work better than others, though, and you should always test your fabric before getting involved in an ambitious project. If you're using synthetic fabric, *don't use a resist—it won't penetrate the fabric* effectively and will just spread on the surface of the fabric.

The resin-based paints add a very slight coating to silk which blocks the silk fibers' transparent and reflective qualities. Therefore, these paints cannot produce the same brilliance and depth of color as the traditional silk painting dyes. A heavy coating of resin-based paints on the silk will also stiffen its fibers somewhat. To counteract this stiffening effect, use a fabric softener in the final wash after the painted fabric has been set.

### PREWASHING COTTON, LINEN AND OTHER FABRICS.

Most fabrics other than silk need to be prewashed to remove finishes so the colors will adhere. Wash cotton with detergent in the washing machine and dry and iron before painting. For blends and synthetics, follow normal washing instructions before painting.

If you plan to paint on pre-sewn garments, we also suggest you prewash and iron them before painting. Avoid fabric softeners; they make it more difficult for the paints to penetrate and adhere to the cloth.

# FOUR
# RESISTS

Liquid dyes and paints flow and move when applied to fabrics. To control this capillary action, a material called a *resist* is used. The use of resist defines the migration of the paints and dyes on fabric for color placement. It is generally used to outline shapes, but when applied with a wide brush, it can also cover larger areas. Resist can be used for open line work, not just to enclose shapes.

The resists generally used in silk painting are gutta serti, both clear and colored, water-based resist, and wax. You can achieve similar results with a few other exotic products such as antifusants. Resists have different properties and you will want to explore them to determine which one is best suited for a particular look.

For the resist to contain the flow of each color within a shape, it *must* completely surround and penetrate every fiber where it is placed.

## Gutta Serti

The French word *serti* means to encircle or surround and is used in conjunction with cloisonné and jewelry, as well as silk painting. We feel this analogy truly describes the beauty of the colors in silk painting, which are surrounded by resist, particularly when the colors have been blended attractively.

Gutta serti is the traditional silk painting resist. Historically, gutta replaced wax in modern silk painting, then the water-soluble resists were developed. Gutta is very effective for silk painting and will give you a sharp, crisp line.

Gutta is rubber- and solvent-based and flammable, so do not work close to an open flame. Keep your containers closed, and ventilate the area. Gutta serti is considered ready to use as purchased, but it has a heavy viscous consistency, and we have found that it works better if you thin it with a small amount of the solvent appropriate for the brand you are using. It does not maintain its balance and needs to be checked regularly. Test the gutta on a strip of fabric before you use it.

Use the appropriate solvent to change the consistency of gutta in accordance with the weight of the fabric. Heavy fabrics need more fluid applications of gutta.

**STORING GUTTA.** Keep gutta in tightly capped containers in a cool dark place and under refrigeration in warm weather. It is difficult to control gutta un-

der certain weather conditions, particularly humidity. Don't let it freeze.

Always store it in the original PVC container, not the applicator, because it will evaporate through the walls of the applicator and dry out. If gutta remains sticky when applied, it has thickened. Add gutta solvent to correct that. If you add too much solvent, keep the container open for a while to let it evaporate. Gutta has a shelf life, depending on the conditions; beyond that point it is ineffective.

**IRONING GUTTA.** When you iron fabric containing gutta, place a sheet of (unprinted) newsprint or old sheeting on the ironing board and one over the fabric, then iron on the *wrong* side. Otherwise gutta will stick to the iron.

After the work is done, you can remove the gutta by dry cleaning the fabric. A faint color will remain, noticeable only when viewed in contrast with white fabric. But you don't necessarily have to remove the gutta. If you leave it on, it will eventually soften with repeated washings and, upon aging, will develop an attractive patina.

## Water-Soluble Resists

Water-soluble resists are clear, colorless, contain no solvents, and are easy to apply. As the name implies, these products are simply washed out with water following the manufacturer's directions. Some wash out in cold water, some in warm water, and some can also be removed by dry cleaning. They don't give you as crisp a line as

**FABRIC SAMPLE**

*Jan Janas*
*Ribbon satin chiffon, dyes, wax resist.*

*The wax resist was applied with a flat bristle brush and a tjanting tool. The dye was painted over the wax.*

**CLOWN**

*(Detail)*

*14″ × 14″  Jan Janas*

*8mm silk, dyes, black gutta, fabric marking pen.*

the gutta serti simply because they are water-soluble—the liquid in the dyes tends to dissolve them if applied too closely. In using them, follow the manufacturer's directions, since handling differs with each brand. We recommend water-soluble resists when working with children in a school environment because they contain no solvents and wash out easily.

Water-soluble resists don't dry as quickly as gutta. They can be used effectively when resisting large areas. They are also particularly good to use with resin-based paints.

**STORING WATER-SOLUBLE RESISTS.** Water-soluble resists are sensitive to the atmosphere and will be rendered ineffective if not properly stored. Store them in a cool, dark place and refrigerate for best results—but don't subject them to freezing. Be aware that these resists have a limited shelf life, so don't buy too much at one time.

## Wax

Wax is also an excellent resist. It gives crisp, sharp lines and holds the dyes back very well. You can successfully paint over this resist. Make sure you remove the droplets of dye left on top of the wax because they will transfer onto your fabric and stain it. You'll find a wealth of information on this resist in books on batik.

At one point, when the gutta and water-soluble resists came into use, the use of wax resist dwindled. But wax is beginning to make a comeback because it is easier to use with silk painting techniques that don't require repeated dipping. You will find more details on wax resist in chapter 12.

To apply the wax, you'll need stiff wide brushes along with a tjanting tool. Heat the wax and apply it to the fabric where you want to maintain the original color. Repeat applications similar to batik.

## Colored Resists

Many artists look for an alternative to the clear lines of the colorless resists. The answer is to use colored resists to add a dramatic dimension to your work. Colored resists are not for the beginner. Using colored resists takes some know-how, the desire to experiment, and the ability to accept that they don't always work perfectly.

**BLACK GUTTA SERTI.** Black gutta serti is most attractive because of the graphic outline it offers. After applying black gutta, place a cloth over the ironing board and over the silk and iron with a hot iron. Black gutta has the advantage that the new formulation is permanent. It's dry-cleanable as well as hand-washable after ironing.

***GOLD AND SILVER GUTTA SERTI.*** Gold and silver gutta serti are also very attractive but *beware*. These resists are fragile and many times will flake off clothing after a short time. You cannot dry-clean fabric that has the metallic guttas on it because the solvents in the dry cleaning process dissolve the gutta, which is the vehicle that holds the metallic flakes to the fabric. Because of these problems, we find the use of gold and silver gutta sertis more appropriate for wall hangings than clothing.

***COLORING CLEAR GUTTA.*** Clear gutta can be colored with printer's ink. Thin a small amount of ink with solvent then add it to the clear gutta. Filter the mixture through a material such as nylon hose to eliminate impurities, and let the colored resist settle overnight. After applying it to the fabric, allow it to cure several days, which will cut down on smearing when the fabric is dry-cleaned. It usually disappears in dry cleaning.

***COLORING WATER-SOLUBLE RESISTS.*** We have discovered that you can color water-soluble resists with silk painting dyes — the dark, intense colors work best. To do this, simply add a *very* small amount of dye to the resist, shake it very well, and allow it to rest. When the dyes you paint with and the dye in the resist are set, the effect is beautiful.

***COLORING WAX.*** Wax can also be colored by melting crayons and blending them into the wax.

## Resist Applicators

Applying resist is one of the skills you'll need to acquire in silk painting. You can apply resists with a variety of tools, each with a different effect: squeeze bottles and other applicators, paper cones, brushes and various objects that will add texture. Use a different applicator for each new resist because the resists are not compatible or mixable with one another.

It's common sense, of course, but when you fill the applicators, remember to place a paper towel over the area you are working on. And never fill the applicators over the silk!

***PLASTIC SQUEEZE BOTTLE.*** The most commonly used and practical applicator is the plastic squeeze bottle — especially when it is fitted with a metal tip for

***COCOON JACKET***
(Detail)
Dominique Bello
Ribbon satin chiffon, French dyes, gutta.

A second design is revealed when resisting and painting on striped textured silks. The flat application of color within the resisted areas draws attention to the light sheer stripes versus the shiny, heavy satin stripe in the fabric.

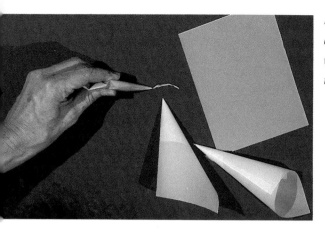

*Paper cones can be filled with thickened dyes or gutta resists. You can obtain very wide or very thin lines by varying the size of the hole in the cone.*

**KIMONO**

(Detail)

Jan Janas

Silk broadcloth, dyes, gold and black resist.

*The gold paint resist, when heat-set with an iron, will not flake off fabric like the metallic guttas do. Because it is a fabric paint resist, it is flexible and will not change the hand of the fabric.*

better control. Metal tips are available in various sizes so you can control the width of the line. To clean the metal applicator tips, soak them in solvent if using gutta serti or rinse them in water if using water-based resists. Use the pin or fine needle that comes with the applicator to keep the opening clear.

**PAPER CONE.** Traditionalists prefer to apply gutta with a paper cone (which doesn't work with the other resists). These cones are made of heavy tracing paper and are similar to the ones used for cake decorating. Use a fine pin or a razor blade to make the opening. Place only a small amount of gutta in the cone at one time or it will come out the top. It takes more skill to apply resists with paper cones, but you can obtain a nice, fine line with them. Of course, the size of the hole will affect the width of your line. Paper cones are particularly good to use with colored guttas. Take your time and apply them carefully. You can store gutta in filled paper cones for a couple of days in a tightly capped jar. Make a whole box full of cones ahead of time so they are ready when you need them.

**USING RESISTS TO ACHIEVE TEXTURE.** For texture, you can use stiff brushes with gutta or water-soluble resists. Polyfoam brushes as well as other objects can also be used with the water-soluble resists in a free-form manner.

# FIVE

# DYES, INKS AND PAINTS

Traditional silk painting dyes come in liquid form ready to use. For the serious amateur and the professional, a mixing palette of the concentrated silk painting dyes is available. They must be diluted. The silk dyes historically have an affinity for silk and wool only, although some artists use them successfully on nylon, spandex, Milliskin and different types of rayons and combinations of those fibers. They are also effective on feathers and leather. It is very important to prewash your fabric and test the dyes on a swatch of the identical fabric you plan to use for your painting. Especially when using a synthetic fabric, you'll find the final results vary considerably.

Silk painting dyes were developed exclusively for fabric painting and have the unique quality of being transparent. These dyes require steam setting to allow them to be hand washed or dry-cleaned. The brilliance of the colors is directly attributed to the steam setting process which allows the colors to "bloom." The dyes bond molecularly to the fabric and become an integral part of it, leaving no residue, therefore the painted fabrics drape beautifully. The dyes are absorbed so evenly into the fabric that it is hard to tell right side from wrong, except on heavy fabrics.

*Note*: Dyes have a limited shelf life and should be stored in a cool, dark place. They are nontoxic, but they usually contain alcohol; sensitive individuals should take precautions, which we will discuss later.

## Characteristics of the Dyes

You will discover as you work with the dyes that each color has certain characteristics, and all are different. Some colors flow in an even manner, some, which are called static, spread less evenly and slower, while others, which are called repelling colors, have the unusual capability to push away other colors, even darker ones, in a very interesting way.

Of course, the characteristics of these dyes vary with different brands and color mixtures. You will discover interesting things as you work with the different color categories mentioned above, particularly the repelling colors, such as yellow, some blues, turquoise and Tyrian pink. When they are applied over colors which are even darker, they push away the original color and claim a territory. We find this fascinating and worth exploring.

**EFFECT OF DYES ON SILK.** When applied to silk, they move easily and that is one of the most exciting

aspects of silk painting. Watching the colors move is an exhilarating experience! The liquid dyes flow on the silk, which means that a spot of color placed on the silk will spread evenly until the fabric has completely absorbed the liquid. They dry very quickly.

As you work with the dyes you will quickly discover that they go a very long way. It is neither necessary nor desirable to overload the fabric. Diluting them, as you often should, allows you to use even less dye and avoid problems such as breaching the lines of resist and excess color run.

Traditional silk painting dyes are available in a broad range of transparent colors. When an area needs to be white, it is simply not painted. The colors intermix easily and can be diluted for paler shades. In addition to direct painting, they can be used for airbrushing, silk screening, stenciling, warp painting, quilting, block printing and stamping.

**EFFECT OF SILK PAINTING DYES ON WOOL.** When you use silk painting dyes on wool, you'll note the following: The dyes flow with more difficulty on wool than on silk because of the nature of the fabric.

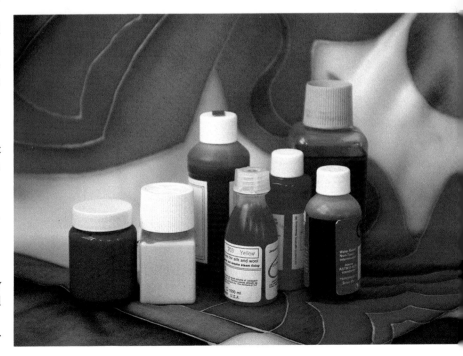

*The fabric artist will find a wide selection of silk dyes, inks and paints in today's art stores and craft shops. Each product has its unique characteristics, so be sure to read the instruction labels before using.*

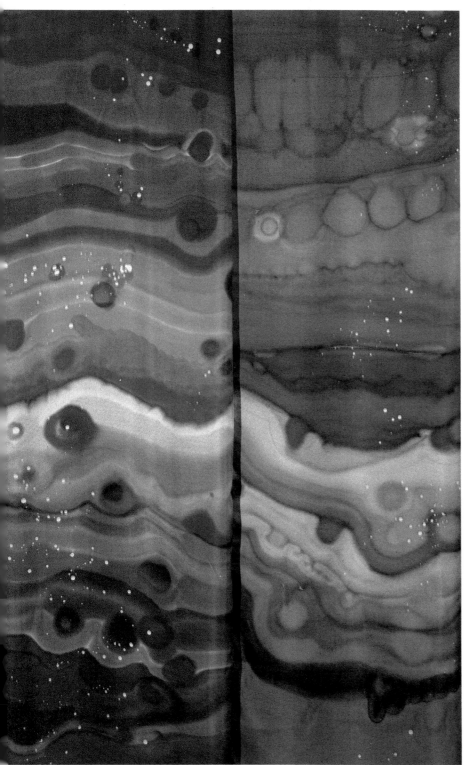

**COLOR CHART PANELS**

*16" × 72" Jan Janas*

**RIGHT:**

*Resin-based paints, broadcloth.*

**LEFT:**

*French dyes, broadcloth.*

*Note the difference in color intensity between the two painted panels. The right panel, painted in resin-based paints, has soft muted hues. The left panel, painted in French dyes, has bright, jewel-like hues. Both liquid colors were applied with a one-inch foam brush. No resist was used and each color brushed on the fabric moved and blended into the previously painted one.*

They dry very slowly. To avoid garish colors on wool, dilute the dyes generously, because the fabric retains a tremendous amount of dye. Painted wools also require a longer steam setting time. (And look out for the smell when steam setting!) Don't let these differences discourage you. Despite all of the above, you will be thrilled with the painted wools. The colors are spectacular in their richness and depth.

**NEW LIQUID RESIN-BASED SILK PAINTS.** These products were a dramatic breakthrough in this art form. They were developed in response to the artists' requests for colors that could be used to paint on *all* fabrics, natural and synthetic, using the authentic silk painting techniques. They are a water-based emulsion of synthetic resins colored by pigments. The resin-based silk paints are not to be confused with the thick acrylic fabric paints because they are liquid and ready to use. (Throughout this book we will refer to these paints as resin-based paints.) The pigments settle, so they must be shaken before use and stirred occasionally while in use. Avoid leaving these paints uncovered for extended periods of time because they dry out. All the colors can be intermixed and can be diluted for paler shades. Clean up is with soap and water. They do not require steam setting and are simply heat-set with an iron. Unlike the silk painting dyes, resin-based paints do not bond molecularly with the fabric. Like other paints, they coat the fibers and give the illusion of a dye. Within minutes after painting they begin to cure. Once they begin this process, you cannot make the dried coat of paint flow again. When the colors are heat-set, the fabrics can be machine washed and dry-cleaned (avoid using harsh detergents), and the painted fabrics will remain soft to the touch.

We have noticed that resin-based paints are quite attractive on 5mm China silk. They do not leave a heavy coat of paint on that weight of silk, although the luster of silk is usually dulled by the resin-based paints. These colors are, however, quite intense on cotton and other fabrics. Like most other silk painting products they are sensitive to intense heat and freezing. They are colorfast, lightfast and nontoxic, which makes them a good choice for working with children and in classroom situations. The liquid resin paints are available in a wide choice of colors and some brands include a white, which is not used to cover but to brighten. They can be used with all traditional silk painting techniques except alcohol.

## *Diluting the Dyes*

Some silk painting dyes are ready to use, but you will often wish to dilute them, particularly the ones that are concentrated. Otherwise the colors will be dull, and you'll get a large amount of color run after setting. To dilute them, you may either use a mixture of water and rubbing alcohol or a concentrated solution of a product called diluent (or more commonly, dilutant). Prepare the diluting solution at least two hours before using and shake. In fact it is a good idea to prepare the solution, label it, and store it in advance. (We recommend you not mix products and brands.)

**ALL-PURPOSE SOLUTION (WATER/ALCOHOL).** A diluting solution of 50 percent water and 50 percent alcohol maintains the correct balance for the dyes to flow effectively. The water is the flowing agent in the solution and the alcohol is the penetrating agent. This solution is basically the correct proportion to deconcentrate dyes. The alcohol of the water/alcohol solution should be ethyl rubbing alcohol. In a pinch, isopropyl alcohol can be substituted. Distilled water is recommended because you will often find chemicals in regular tap water that might affect the dyes. If you use only water to

**SILK SCARF**

*12" × 60"  Pennie Miller*
*8mm silk, dyes, silk-screened.*

The whole scarf was wet down with the diluent. Diluted orange dye was applied to each end of the scarf with gradations using a clean foam brush toward the center. The scarf was dried. The basic design element in the scarf is the repeated triangle, which was outlined with resist. The dark areas were then filled in.

**FISH**

*14" × 14"  Jan Janas*
*8mm silk, resin-based paints, clear resist, salt.*

The curing factor of the resin-based paints was an advantage in this painting. The subtle textural lines in the background were applied after the turquoise had cured, therefore no dark edge line appeared. Once the threads of the fabric have a cured coat of paint on them, the paint will inhibit the movement of additional applications of liquid color allowing fine detailing.

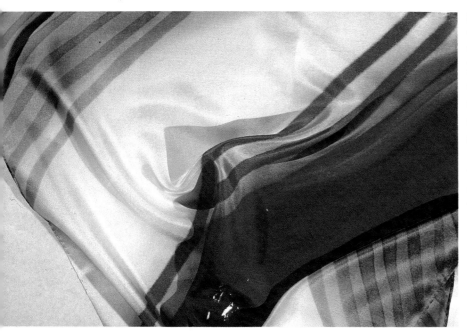

**SILK SCARF**

*12" × 60"  Pennie Miller*

*8mm silk, dyes, antifusant.*

*The scarf was evenly coated with an antifusant and let dry. Dye was then painted in stripes on the scarf using various-sized brushes. While the dye was still damp, a large foam brush with diluent in it was quickly and lightly brushed across the dye. All white areas between the stripes became pastel as the foam brush picked up color from the previously painted dye on the stripes.*

dilute the colors, you might notice that sometimes, something happens to the colorants in the dyes. They do not penetrate the fabric and the water will continue to flow on its surface. You might see brushstrokes, light and dark areas, and water rings on your painting.

For very light pastel colors, use a mixture of one part water and three parts alcohol. (This will give you less of a breakdown of color than using equal parts of each.) Slowly add the dyes to this pastel diluting solution. You should be aware that if you dilute certain colors too much, they will lose their body, streak, and get a washed-out look.

For best results when you are diluting concentrated dyes, stir them well because you're mixing two solutions of different densities and you will need to attain the proper homogeneity.

In general you are dealing with several different concentrations of color for the dyes:

- Pure colors that are used as is, except for very concentrated dyes which must be deconcentrated before they are diluted.
- Medium colors that are diluted at a proportion of approximately 80 percent pure color to 20 percent diluting solution.
- Light colors that are made up of 50 percent medium color and 50 percent pastel solution.
- Pastel colors that are made up of 20 percent of the light color and 80 percent of the pastel solution.

**OTHER SOLUTIONS.** Certain brands of dyes have concentrates that are used in place of the water/alcohol

solution. They are a good choice if you do not wish to use alcohol. You must add seven times the volume of water to the concentrate to prepare the solution. It is odorless and foams when mixed. Because it contains no alcohol, it slows down the drying time of the dyes and allows you to work at a somewhat slower pace. It is also effective in getting smoother surfaces with a minimum of streaking.

One disadvantage is that the salt effect is sometimes less dramatic when you use these prepared diluents. And be aware that if you use them straight, without dilution, your colors will disappear.

**DILUTING FABRIC PAINTS.** So far, we have been discussing ways to dilute silk painting dyes. For the fabric paints, use the special diluting solution—not alcohol, because these paints don't contain alcohol. This diluent is also a concentrate and needs to be diluted with seven times the volume of water. It is preferable to use this solution instead of water because it maintains the lightfastness of the colors. Fabric paints are less vibrant on silk, so start out by diluting as little as possible until you get a feel for the proportions. These paints are quite bright on fabrics such as cotton.

We think this information is helpful, particularly if you are working with your colors in a very precise way. However, if you feel comfortable working in a more relaxed and imprecise way, and aren't afraid to experiment, this information will bring more variety to your artwork.

## Cleaning Up

Dye spills on your clothing or other surfaces can sometimes be cleaned up if done immediately. The traditional silk painting dyes can be removed more effectively when the fabric they're spilled on is not silk or wool. First use alcohol, then the appropriate cleaners for the fabric. The paints adhere well to all fabrics though, so protect your clothes accordingly. Try soap and water or diluent. To avoid staining your hands, use gloves, or be sure that your hands are not dry—the dyes adhere more insistently to dry skin. Warm water, soap and a scrub brush are quite effective to clean your hands but the dyes tend to stain the nails. Liquid organic cleansers are helpful for removing dyes from your hands.

# BRUSHES AND OTHER APPLICATORS

The best tool for applying the dyes depends on the size of the area you wish to cover, the intricacy of the design, and the cost of the brushes. Your selection of applicators is also affected by the size of your budget and your style of silk painting. Here are some of the advantages and disadvantages of the applicators and brushes we tried and their varied uses.

**SQUIRREL HAIR BRUSHES.** Squirrel hair brushes, which are watercolor-type quills, are unquestionably the best for silk painting. Their only drawback is the cost. On the other hand, we feel that they're well worth the investment, since you'll be using them for a long, long time and, with proper care, they should last. Squirrel hair brushes have a nice wide belly and come to an exquisite point. Because of their wide belly, squirrel hair brushes hold a generous quantity of liquid without dripping. When you're attempting to gently push dyes into tiny spaces, you will discover how effective that point can be.

**QUILLS.** Quills are available in several sizes but we have found sizes #1 and #2 the most useful. These brushes are very versatile. They can cover a wide area and still be used in very fine detail work because of the extra fine point. They work very well for multiple loading and blending.

**WATERCOLOR BRUSHES.** Watercolor brushes of all types are also good for silk painting. Always test the brush by purchasing one before you invest in several. It should be soft, responsive and have no stray hairs. It should also hold a substantial amount of color without dripping and still keep a good point.

A good sable brush is excellent for fine detail work and, because it is firmer than the quill, it is particularly good for dry-brush work.

**BAMBOO BRUSHES.** Inexpensive bamboo brushes tend to have stray hairs and are difficult to keep pointed while painting. But many silk painters like them, so you may wish to have some on hand.

**FAN BRUSHES.** The fan brush is a useful tool for silk painting. It is not useful for applying large amounts of color to the fabric but for creating special effects such as dry-brushing and texturing.

**FOAM BRUSHES.** For large backgrounds, foam brushes are best. They're inexpensive and can hold

a large quantity of liquid. They are available in one-, two- and three-inch sizes. Anything larger than that is too heavy when loaded and will drip on your fabric. We prefer the ones with a wooden handle because its stiff inner core allows you to paint more easily.

**BRUSHES FOR WAX RESISTS.** If you work with wax, you'll need inexpensive brushes of nylon, pork bristles or any material that can withstand the heat involved in using the wax. Don't worry about leaving wax in the brush. It will harden, but once you put the brush in the hot wax, it will soften again.

**BRUSHES FOR WATER-SOLUBLE RESISTS.** For water-soluble resists, try using a fan brush or stiff brushes for a textured look. Scrubber-type brushes are practical when painting with resin-based fabric paints on cotton garments such as shirts and sweatshirts.

**COTTON SWABS.** Cotton swabs are useful for testing and selecting colors for a project. Use a clean one every time you dip into another color. The cotton swabs with a plastic center work better than the cardboard ones. They're also great for a quick "pick up" when there's a break in the resist line and for scrubbing an uneven area.

**AIRBRUSHES.** An airbrush can be used quite successfully for silk painting, too, but that is beyond the scope of this book. However, there are ways of applying dyes in an airbrush manner. You can use an atomizer, sprayer or a spritzer bottle. More about this in the misting section of chapter 17.

**BRUSHES**

*Your choice of what brush to use for silk painting is going to depend a lot on your personal painting style and what silk painting technique you are going to use on the fabric.*

***CLEANING YOUR BRUSH***

*Stroke the brush on a bar of mild soap and then twirl it in a circular motion in the palm of your hand. You may need to repeat this step several times until the rinse water runs clean.*

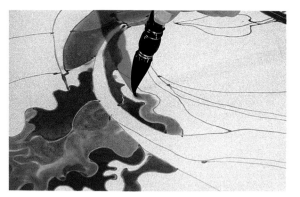

## How to Use the Brushes

It's better to have fewer brushes of better quality to be used for specific purposes. You'll notice quality brushes contain a sizing to protect them. To gently break the stiffness of this sizing, rinse in lukewarm water and soap. Keep doing this until the brush feels soft.

Prepare two containers with clean water, one to wash and one to rinse your brushes in. It is not always necessary to clean your brushes between colors, because you will obtain unusual effects when you have several colors on your brush at the same time.

**HANDLING BRUSHES.** Always prewet your brushes with water about fifteen minutes before you start to paint. This will give you a more even application from the start. *Never leave the brush with its head down in the water.* This is deadly to the brush and will affect its performance. Foam brushes will become waterlogged.

After you have wet the brush and let it rest for a few minutes, pick up some color, using approximately half the brush. Remove some of the excess color by pressing the brush on the side of the container. *Stroke* the excess color off the brush on paper towels. Use this technique of stroking off the excess dye until you get a good feel for how much liquid you are picking up with the brush.

Start painting by placing the brush in the center of a resisted shape and lightly *stroking* the color toward the lines of resist. Pick up more color before your brush is too dry, or you will get uneven areas. Dip the brush often to obtain even distribution of color. When the brush is loaded correctly, the area on which you place your brush should approximately double in size.

**FOAM BRUSHES AND APPLICATORS.** When working with foam brushes and applicators, prewet them

and squeeze the extra moisture out before you use them. They hold a substantial amount of color so be sure to press the excess off on the edge of the container before you start to paint. When you have finished painting, wear gloves to rinse your foam brushes well by squeezing them under running water until it runs clear. Place them foam side up in a container to dry. They can be reused many times. Be sure you keep one exclusively for water/alcohol solution or water to avoid any color contamination.

**CLEANING AND STORING YOUR BRUSHES.** When you have finished painting, do not allow your brush to dry without rinsing the color out. Rinse in lukewarm water—never hot. Stroke the brush on a bar of soap or use neutral shampoo, then twirl it in a circular motion in the palm of your hand. Repeat this step several times until the water runs clear. You may need to work at it harder when using the resin-based fabric paints which leave a very light film on the brushes. You can then rinse the brush in water/alcohol solution or in plain alcohol if the dyes were used.

Remember that rinsing is not enough to clean the brushes and never leave them soaking in water because they will become waterlogged and deteriorate. A dirty brush will give you an unpleasant surprise when you try to use it the next time. The residue from the dirty brush will get deposited on the fabric, will stain it, and muddy the color you are using. An ugly aureola or halo often develops in this case.

After rinsing the brush, shape it and allow it to dry on the side of a table so the hairs hang over the edge. You can then store it bristles up or laying flat only. If you are not planning to use your natural hair brushes for a while, be sure that you store them with some mothballs or cedar chips because the moths love your brushes too!

***PAINTING IN A RESISTED AREA***

*Lightly stroke the liquid color toward the lines of resist. In small resisted areas, you need only to touch down on the silk with the tip of your brush. The capillary action of the liquid colors on the silk will evenly fill the space with color.*

# 2 Basic Working Procedures

*This section deals with the broader aspects of silk painting, previewing the basic processes in a general sense. We recommend that you read the entire book before you start your first project to become familiar with the terms and techniques involved. You may also find this a handy book to keep by your side as you work, to refer to when you hit a snag.*

*This section reflects the sequence of steps, more or less in order: planning the design of the painting, general information about color and color mixing, ways to handle the background, how to stretch fabric over a frame, and essential information about setting dyes. While this book stresses silk painting with traditional silk painting dyes, which require steam setting, we also discuss the new resin-based paints, other ways of setting these paints, and handling the newer materials.*

*While we want you to keep an open mind, as we do, we cannot help but note the vast difference in the final results when using the traditional materials versus the newest ones on the market, and express our strong preference for the traditional silk painting dyes. But the spirit of this book is experimentation and discovery, and we urge you to experiment and see for yourself which materials and methods you prefer.*

**DESIGNING FROM NATURE**

*Generally a drawing from nature will be more original than one observed in a photograph. One good drawing of a single flower can be repeated many times within the same composition. Change the look of the flower by adding new colors, varying its placement in the composition, overlapping mirroring images, and simplifying.*

The first step in painting on silk is choosing a design that appeals to you or the person you're painting for. You'll also have to know how the finished piece will be used so the type of fabric and technique chosen will be appropriate. After those decisions have been made, carefully think through how you will create your painting. Don't forget to consider the color combinations, possible techniques, and the inherent limitations of your particular fabric choice.

Don't feel intimidated if you can't draw. Many techniques don't require drawing ability, and once you develop a feel for good color combinations, the rest will come easily. On the other hand, drawing your own designs is not as difficult as it might appear. Geometric and abstract shapes can be used to create beautiful paintings. If you start out with pencil and paper (or felt-tip marker or other medium) and just keep drawing, you'll soon develop the skill. To help you, here are some basics.

## The Basics of Good Design

To create a pleasing composition, you need balance, repetition, and a variety of sizes, shapes and colors. Creating the illusion of distance will add depth and dimension to your work. You'll also need a focal point, which should be as attractive and appealing as possible.

Design inspiration can come from many sources. Look into the principles of flower arranging, which can help you develop design skills and a feel for using colors. Look around you with an open mind. Notice shapes in nature, fabric and

wallpaper designs, magazine illustrations, and works of art by the masters. Your observations will become a wealth of ideas you can incorporate into your own work.

You'll soon discover certain types of designs are more successfully translated into silk paintings than others. Florals have a general appeal, as do Art Deco motifs, abstracts and stained glass. Ethnic designs, geometrics and bold shapes are also very adaptable to silk painting.

Try to translate what you envision and dream of onto silk. You don't need to have a specific design in mind. Start a folder of ideas that appeal to you, but be careful not to copy designs that are not in the public domain or specifically published for copying. (Copyright laws are quite specific.) Your idea folder should include eye-catching color combinations and interesting illustrations that, with a few changes, will become unique designs ready to be adapted to silk painting.

As you work with silk painting and its various applications, you will develop your own style, and this will be very exciting. But beware of becoming too stultified and repetitive. Don't allow yourself to be trapped by past prejudices about colors, color combinations, techniques or inhibitions. Keep trying different styles and techniques.

To help you judge your design for an important project, paint a small sample and study the colors and other design elements. Steam set the sample to get the true intensity of the colors.

## Simple Designs

Begin your silk painting exploration with simple shapes, like leaf outlines, geometrics, free form and florals, manipulating them to suit your needs. Simplicity is of the essence! Stay away from small, intricate shapes. Break down your backgrounds into smaller areas—it's sometimes difficult to achieve an even color when you have to paint quickly in all directions to avoid a dark edge line. Suggestions like this will become obvious rather quickly once you begin.

With a simple design, you can use various techniques to enhance the project and avoid the flat look often found in silk paintings where colors are applied as solid-color shapes. To avoid a paint-by-number look, personalize your design by using your skill and technical knowledge to break the monotony of these flat shapes and create a dynamic work of art. See the technique sections such as salt and alcohol in Part Three.

## Handling Intricate Designs

The most important elements in a silk painting are the design and the color combinations. For instance, if you design an exotic bird in the middle of a lush tropical forest, you can easily fill in every nook and cranny of your surface with interesting shapes. It will look busy, but that is what you set out to achieve—just be sure a complicated design doesn't overwhelm your painting. It is up to you to break down the details in a pleasing way and to use your colors judiciously to create a unified whole. In this instance, we suggest you limit your palette of colors, vary their intensity, and create contrast by changing the size of the shapes.

## Free-form Techniques

Movement, play of color, and mood are the hallmark of these silk painting techniques. We'll describe many of them in detail in future chapters, such as how to use salt, alcohol, watercolor, wet-on-wet, colored backgrounds, pre-resisted surfaces, and free-flowing blended yardage to create beautiful paintings. For these techniques, a good design is critical, particularly when juxtaposing shapes and colors without resist. As suggested earlier in this section, take your inspiration from nature, architecture, unusual photographs and abstract art. Sketch your designs on paper with colored markers or some other medium to help you visualize your ideas.

One good exercise is to try your hand at a monochromatic (*camaïeu*, in French) silk painting. The painting is done with different values of

one color arranged in a pleasing way and maybe incorporating various techniques. Monochromes are challenging, but fun to do.

## The Design Outline

Most of us feel comfortable using a design that has been traced rather than painting freehand. To begin, use sturdy tracing paper and a wide *waterproof* black marker. The paper needs to be sturdy so you can easily roll it, store it, and reuse it. If you're copying a design and the size is not correct for the project, use the simple method of squaring off the design with graph paper and adjust it to suit your purpose. The use of a photocopy machine makes enlarging a design easy. When work-

### SQUARING OFF THE DESIGN

*Sometimes your sketch for a piece of work is difficult to enlarge in correct proportions. Here's a simple method: measure and draw a grid of squares on your sketch and then duplicate this grid in double or triple proportions (example: a one-inch square on a sketch may equal a two-inch square on an enlargement) on a larger sheet of paper. Number the grid squares on the sketch and on the large sheet of paper to keep track of the area you're drawing in.*

### DIVORCE TULSA STYLE

(Detail)
45" × 108"  Jan Janas
5mm silk, resin-based paints, black and gold resist.

*In this painting, the palette of colors was limited and their intensity varied. Contrast was created by changing the size of the shapes. Symbols, words and abstracted figures fill the entire surface of the fabric. The soft, smooth blends of color help tie the many shapes together. Look for the small, interesting details.*

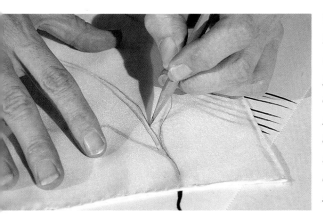

**TRANSFERRING YOUR DESIGN**

*If you are going to paint on a light-weight silk—5mm, 8mm, 10mm— you can lay your stretched material directly on top of the pattern and trace your design on the silk. If it is an intricate design, tape the silk down on the pattern so it will not move. This is especially important if you have long straight lines to trace.*

ing with a simple design, make broad lines with a black marker for the large, important shapes. Leave out the details; they can be added later in the painting process. When using free-form techniques such as alcohol, salt, or color simply blended and placed next to another color, first make a few small test projects to scale to discover what appeals to you.

**TRANSFERRING THE DESIGN.** There are different methods of transferring a design, depending on the weight of the fabric and the method you prefer. Often you can trace it directly from the pattern onto the fabric with the resist.

To transfer your design, stretch the silk over the frame and place it over the design. (See pages 41-44 on stretching silk.) If you can clearly see the design, and you feel comfortable doing it, trace the design with resist directly onto the silk. You might bring the design closer, but do not tape it too closely because the resist might smear and stick when it comes in contact with the design.

**SHELLS AND CRAB**

*14" × 14" Jan Janas*

*8mm silk, resin-based paints, clear resist.*

*In this painting, the design was free-handed in with clear resist. The resist was used not only to outline the shapes, but also to enhance the textural and graphic qualities of each shape. The resist was applied quickly to keep a sketch-like look to the painting. Notice the resist line has high contrast in its width: thick and thin.*

*Charcoal on heavy fabric.* If the fabric is so heavy that you absolutely cannot see the design underneath, use very fine charcoal to trace the outline on tracing paper, then flip the paper over with the charcoal lines touching the fabric. Retrace the design with a smooth-tipped tool such as the back end of a pen. Be sure you've drawn the design in reverse so it transfers right side up. After applying the resist you can shake the dust off.

There are also other approaches if your design is simple, with bold shapes. You can use cutouts as your guide. Or, when the design is a free technique, you can poke pins straight down into the fabric at strategic locations and use them as guides to keep you within your design.

If you prefer to transfer the design onto the fabric, you can use soft-colored pastel pencils. We do not recommend pencils unless you test them thoroughly, because they usually get locked on the fabric by the resist, and they do not come out when the resist is removed. Do *not* use pens with disappearing ink because, in time, the ink will disintegrate the fabric.

*Gutta resist.* Some silk painting artists use the following method successfully when using gutta resist. Take a piece of glass and elevate it off the work surface by placing four objects of the same height at each corner, then place a light underneath the glass. Place the design you are tracing on heavy tracing paper on the glass and tape the silk over the design. Use the gutta resist and outline the design. When the resist is dry, peel the paper design away from the silk. (We believe that this method is successful because the heat from the lamp dries the gutta quickly, so it does not spread.)

*A caution on straight lines.* If you trace straight lines on fabric while the fabric is stretched, they may be distorted in your finished painting, so trace straight lines before you stretch the silk. (The kinds of lines to trace are found in a scarf with a border, large geometric shapes, and stripes.) When you stretch the fabric, the lines will not appear to be straight. Apply the resist on the distorted lines. They will be straight again when the silk is removed from the frame.

If you can trace a design freehand, this is really the easiest way to proceed. Explore the various design possibilities and consider combinations of various techniques. Just remember, while it is important to use a variety of techniques to avoid monotony, knowing when to stop is an art in itself!

# WORKING WITH COLOR

Now we come to the most important element: *color*! In silk painting you will have an immediate emotional response to the most glorious colors you can imagine. They are incredibly vibrant, shiny and explosive. They can be bold, or they can be subtle and quiet. We all have a personal response to the colors around us, including those in landscapes, houses, and in the clothes and accessories we wear. Subconsciously, we are constantly making color choices that affect our lives, creating an atmosphere and image that's uniquely our own. We go along with fashion colors, but we deal with them on a personal level of preference, quickly realizing that some just do not work for us individually. We have to assert our color sense because color *demands* our attention.

By taking you through the basics of color, we hope to help you develop the necessary skills to create successful color combinations that will speak to you and to those around you. As surface designers, we feel understanding the basics of color behavior and color mixing will give you a good foundation for working with dyes and liquid paints to develop your own design.

## What Is Color?

What we call *color* is actually light waves being reflected or absorbed by an object. Each light wave can be perceived by our eye as a recognizable *hue* (an identifiable color like red or blue). Color can also be measured by *intensity* (brightness or dullness of a color) and *value* (its degree of lightness or darkness).

## The Color Wheel

To visualize how colors relate to one another, we suggest you purchase a color wheel from an art supply store. Study the wheel and actually paint all of its color combinations as an exercise. Read the following text on changing intensity, value and color temperature, and practice those basic ways of handling color as well. This will give you a working knowledge of the way colors work. Following are some color wheel basics:

• The *primary* colors are red-yellow-blue. They are called primary because they cannot be made from a mixture of other colors; they are basic.
• Mix two primaries to get *secondary* colors: orange-green-violet.
• Mix a primary with a neighboring secondary to get *tertiary* colors: red-orange, yellow-orange, yellow-green, blue-green, blue-violet, red-violet.

**SILKSCAPES: FACES**

*Alison Abbott and Lynn Weinberg*
*Silk scarf, 14mm crepe de Chine, French dyes, black resist.*

*The bold application of pure colors and black resist outlined in this painting have a powerful impact on the viewer. The wide border of repeated colored dots is balanced with the larger center shapes of abstracted faces.*

**REDUCING INTENSITY.** The color wheel will also help you visualize *complementary* colors which are hues that appear opposite each other on the color wheel. Violet is the complement of yellow, green is the complement of red, and orange is the complement of blue. In color mixing, adding a color to its complement will make it more neutral by turning it brown or gray. In other words, adding a color to its complement will reduce the color's *intensity*. For example, to dull a blue (change the intensity) without changing its value (not darkening it), add a small amount of orange to it.

**CHANGING THE VALUE.** To make all hues *darker* or *lighter* in value, add black to darken them and white or a clear extender (water or diluent) to lighten

**COLOR WHEEL**

*Just by mixing the primary colors (reds, yellows, blues) plus black, white, or water in various proportions, you will be able to produce any color you can possibly imagine for your silk painting.*

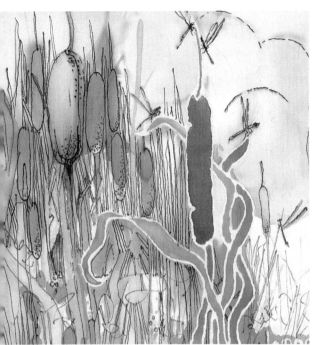

**CATTAILS**

14" × 14"  Jan Janas
Broadcloth, resin-based paints, clear
and black resist.

Clear resist was used only on the cattail
in the foreground. Black paint was used
on the cattail to darken the value of the

brown to give the illusion of dimension.
The black was repeatedly diluted for
balance. Water-diluted colors loosely
painted in the background suggest other
cattail shapes, water and sky. Some
areas were left unpainted. When the
painting was dry, black resist was used
to sketch in details.

them. Black will also dull a color and white or clear
extender will brighten a color, which means the intensity as well as the value is affected by adding
white or black.

**COLOR TEMPERATURE.** Colors also have visual temperature—*warm* or *cool*. Generally the colors associated with summer or fire are warm: reds, oranges
and yellows. Colors associated with winter or water
are cool: blues, greens and violets.

To cool a color, therefore, you can add a touch
of blue, green or violet to it, and to warm a color,
add a touch of red, orange or yellow. By changing
the temperature of the color, especially neutrals
like grays and browns, you can create very subtle
movements and color combinations in your design.

## Color Schemes

Color schemes are planned combinations of colors
that help create color unity within a design. The
schemes are predictable and can be formulated;

however, colors are creative tools. The ultimate
guide for color choice within your design should
be the colors' emotional effect rather than strict
adherence to a color scheme.

The traditional color schemes are:

*1.* **Monochromatic.** One color plus black and
white.

*2.* **Complementary.** A primary color and its complement—for example, red and green, blue and
orange, yellow and violet.

*3.* **Split Complements.** A primary color plus the
tertiary colors on either side of its complement. For
example:

   **A.** red, blue-green, yellow-green
   **B.** blue, red-orange, yellow-orange
   **C.** yellow, blue-violet, red-violet

*4.* **Analogous:** Closely related hues on the color
wheel. For example:

   **A.** red, red-orange, red-violet
   **B.** orange, red-orange, yellow-orange
   **C.** yellow, yellow-orange, yellow-green
   **D.** green, yellow-green, blue-green
   **E.** blue, blue-green, blue-violet
   **F.** violet, blue-violet, red-violet

*5.* **Triadic:** Any three colors placed equidistant
from each other in a triangle formation on the color
wheel, e.g.:

   **A.** red-yellow-blue
   **B.** green-violet-orange
   **C.** red-violet, blue-green, yellow-orange
   **D.** blue-violet, yellow-green, red-orange

Knowing the traditional color schemes will give
you a point of departure. By varying the value,
intensity and temperature of each hue, you can
create an infinite variety of hues within a set
scheme.

**ABSTRACT**

4" × 4"  Jan Janas
8mm silk, dyes, gutta.

This painting was an exercise to practice
the even blend technique. The complementary color scheme of blue and
orange was used. Notice how the intensity of the orange changes as blue is
blended into it.

## Colors on Silk

Several points to remember when working with liquid colors on silk: transparent colors dry lighter than they appear when wet; always mix dark colors *into* light colors; make color test swatches on bits of the same fabric that your design is going to be painted on.

**MANIPULATING COLOR.** Once you've learned how to mix any color you wish, your next step is to understand how to create certain effects on your silk. By varying the temperature, value and intensity of a color, you can visually manipulate the size, mood, distance and contrast in your designs. For example, here are some basics. Warm, light and bright colors tend to increase the size of objects within a design. These types of colors also advance and attract more attention.

There are also subtle emotional responses and symbolism attached to color. In terms of warm colors they are:

*Red:* Attention, stop (like the stoplight), magic, hot, fire, erotic, excitement, strength, war, love, anger.

*Orange:* Cheerful, luminous, warmth, fall, friendly, urban, energy.

*Yellow:* Spiritual, wisdom, oriental, sun, joy, happiness, summer, prejudice, cowardice, caution.

Also, bright colors stand out more when painted next to their complements or when used with grays or browns.

On the other hand, cool, dark, dull colors tend to recede in a design. Cool objects also appear to decrease in size and are relaxing. Some of the emotional responses and symbolism attached to cool colors are:

*Blues:* Sky, cool, restful, water, devotion, conservation, control, moody, sad, patience, maternal.

*Green:* Go (like the stoplight), environment, nature, growth, balance, suburban, envy.

*Violets:* Royalty, culture, elegant, quiet, dusk.

To create interest in a design or to project contours of shapes, consider emphasizing *contrast* by varying the visual temperature, value and/or intensity of a color rather than by introducing a new color.

Remember, you can learn about color only by working with it. After a time, and trial and error, you will begin to experience an intuitive understanding of color and will capture the essence of each piece of work you create.

**SEA ANEMONES**

(Detail)

12" × 60"  Jan Janas

8mm silk, dyes, fabric marking pen, salt.

This painting uses a complementary color scheme of yellows and purples dropped onto the scarf with droppers. Different types of salt crystals were strategically placed on the wet colors.

**SILK SCARF**

12" × 60"  Pennie Miller

8mm silk, French dyes, resist, alcohol.

This monochromatic uses madder throughout at different values. Black resist delineates the borders. The outer border, first painted with a dark value, is spotted with a paler version that acts as a repelling color. The middle value is left plain while the inside shape is spotted with alcohol.

**POPPY SILK SCARF**

(Detail)

24" × 24"  Jan Janas

8mm silk, French dye, clear gutta.

A very small quantity of green was added to its complementary color, red, and red to the green, which "cuts" the colors so it tones and unifies them. Initially the design was outlined with clear resist.

**ALLEY CATS**

14" × 14"  Jan Janas

8mm silk, dyes, black gutta.

Above is an example of how the frame and background can be used to make the characters stand out. The yellow, red and blue colors are based on the triadic color scheme.

**LIZARD**

14" × 14"  Jan Janas

8mm silk, French dyes, water-soluble resist.

Movement is illustrated here by color placement. The head of the lizard is surrounded with red, in the direction he seems to be moving, while the darker shade in the back recedes.

Silk painting dyes dry so quickly that applying backgrounds is something you should approach with knowledge and respect! Backgrounds—in addition to being just plain and beautifully flat, light or dark—can be graduated, painted wet-on-wet, striped or watercolored, salted, stippled with alcohol or color, painted over or under antifusants. A background, by the skill of application, the selection of colors, and technique can make or break a work of art.

The background is usually planned as part of the overall decisions that are made before work starts. Leaving this decision to the last minute can be disastrous. On the other hand, sometimes as work progresses, your initial decisions don't work well and a quick change of plan may be necessary. When this occurs, and you stop liking the direction your work is moving, as a rule, your instincts are probably correct. As your skills develop you will feel surer of the backgrounds you choose for silk painting.

## Types of Backgrounds

There are four broad categories of background: the background applied around a resisted design; the background painted before the resist is applied; the background applied when the fabric is wet; the background applied when the fabric is dry.

Keep your work area free of excessive heat and drafts. Traditional silk painting dyes dry very fast. Capillary action allows them to flow easily and quickly on the fabric, and this characteristic is important to achieving a beautiful design. Heat and drafts can dry your dyes too quickly, robbing your design of its fluid, spontaneous quality. The resin-based paints move more slowly than dyes and dry even more quickly. So adjust your technique and work area accordingly and sometimes consider working wet-on-wet for more efficient application of even backgrounds. Finally, be sure you use fabric that has been properly prepared for painting as explained in chapter 3.

## How to Apply Backgrounds

When you plan a painting, you need to decide the color of the background and the overall effect of the design. You may want a neutral background so the design stands out, or you may want to feature the background and create a design that enhances it. Try painting a few samples on scrap fabric or paper to better visualize your idea.

**DAY LILIES**
(Detail)
11" × 48"   Jan Janas
8mm silk, dyes, antifusant.

This is a typical example of a background that was "recaptured." The value of the original orange background clashed with the delicate design and did not allow it to stand out. The problem was remedied by painting the background with a flat black. Some of the orange shows through because antifusant was already down and the black was brushed on at different angles within the design.

The background color is usually applied last, particularly if it is the darker color. This is an advantage—it will allow you to hide any problem painting areas. There are other tips on painting backgrounds that you should keep in mind:

• A simple flat background requires thought and swift application. In painting backgrounds, it is *critical* that you paint quickly, without stopping. Prepare an adequate amount of dye, have paper towels close by, and take the phone off the hook! If you're new at doing backgrounds, plan a design that requires painting several small background areas, separated by lines of resist. This is easier than working on large areas.

• Narrow areas between lines of resist tend to dry lighter than large areas of solid color.

• On dry fabric, paint the background by applying bands of color with a generously loaded brush. Reload the brush frequently and paint with overlapping strokes. Always allow the liquid colors to migrate toward the lines of resist in both directions. Fill in with additional color if the dye does not migrate all the way to the line.

• If you have chosen to place your design in the center of an area, you will need to proceed as above, but you will have to paint the background on both sides of the design simultaneously, so they remain wet at all times.

• If the colors are diluted, adding more alcohol (about 40 percent water and 60 percent alcohol) to the solution will help you apply the dyes more evenly. Although the dyes even out as they dry, you may wish to rub paper towels over a background wash to smooth out streaked areas.

• Much of this information also applies to the resin-based paints, but instead of alcohol you will be using the appropriate diluting solution and will need to scrub the background with a foam brush.

**GRADUATED BACKGROUNDS.** A graduated background can be done in different ways. Some artists prefer to start with the light colors and move on to the darker ones while others prefer the reverse.

A general way to proceed is as follows: if you are planning a white area, paint it with the water/alcohol solution. The water/alcohol solution will act as a mild resist. Begin painting the color furthest from the white area and paint the successive colors by overlapping and keeping the areas well blended and wet. As the colors become lighter and approach the wet area painted with the water/alcohol solution, allow them to blend into the water. Gently

scrub with a clean cotton swab or large clean brush if necessary. Using the same technique, you can place the lightest area at the top, center or sides of your work.

**WET-ON-WET AND WATERCOLOR BACKGROUNDS.** Wet-on-wet and watercolor backgrounds require essentially the same technique. Wet the background down with wetting agent (water/alcohol) solution to keep it as wet as possible as you work, or run a very light wash of color over the area first, then apply the colors quickly, in a fluid manner. Note that the colors float on the solution and can be shifted to obtain a pleasing background. When you are pleased with the result, stop the action of the colors quickly with a hair dryer. Otherwise they will keep moving and you may be disappointed. Start the drying at the corners and work toward the center.

**PANSIES**

14" × 14"  Jan Janas
8mm silk, dyes, clear resist.

The shapes behind the flowers discreetly break down the background so it could be worked easily and effectively. The shading around the petals pushes the flowers into the foreground.

**BUTTERFLIES**

(Detail)
Jan Janas
8mm silk, dyes, resist, alcohol.

There are many intriguing ways to show movement in silk paintings. In this instance, the wavy alcohol lines create the moiré effect and combine with the stippling to show movement of air and depth around the butterflies. Shading is also effective in this combination.

**SALT ON BACKGROUNDS.** Salt can be used in a background to create a halo around a resisted shape, to hide a problem, or just to add interest to a plain design. (See chapter 15 for more on this technique.) Apply the background color with one hand and salt the wet background swiftly with the other so as not to interrupt the application of the background color.

**ALCOHOL AND DYES.** Stippling with alcohol or dyes can bring a background to life. Stippling is also effective in connecting shapes that would otherwise appear disconnected. After the background is dry, use a very dry brush dipped in concentrated dye and add touches for relief. Alcohol is also effective, but for the resin-based paints, use water or diluent.

**SKY BACKGROUNDS.** Sky backgrounds are obtained by swirling the brush on the silk and creating light and dark areas such as to depict a stormy sky. The same effect is also achieved by using alcohol to swirl.

**STRIPED BACKGROUNDS.** Stripes can be very effective in backgrounds. Soft-edged or blended stripes can be merged into each other by scrubbing their edges or by working on top of a water/alcohol solution base that will keep the fabric wet so the striped edges remain soft. If you want hard-edged stripes, draw lines of resist of different widths in the background of a resisted design. This is particularly effective with black resist because of its strong graphic appeal. The remainder of the design will need to be lighter in value to balance the strong horizontal or vertical lines. Needless to say great skill for straight resist line application is a must in this case!

**HALO EFFECT.** A halo effect is effective and attractive in backgrounds. To make a halo, place the water/alcohol solution around a resisted shape, apply colors to the wet area, and allow them to gently blend. Try this with salt for a delicate effect. Both techniques really bring a design to life.

**ANTIFUSANTS IN BACKGROUNDS.** Another possibility for backgrounds is using color in combination with antifusants (see chapter 13). A colored wash can be placed on the fabric first, then the antifusant is applied before you actually begin painting. A small quantity of dye or paint can be added to the antifusant to softly color the background, or a prepared surface can be misted.

*SILK SCARF*

*(Detail)*

*30" × 30"  Jan Janas*

*8mm silk, dyes, gutta, antifusant.*

*The flowers and leaves were resisted and the hummingbirds were coated with antifusant, then painted with color. The background was dampened with the alcohol solution and then the gray color was quickly swirled on the silk with a one-inch foam brush to create light and dark areas of contrast.*

***QUICKLY STOPPING THE ACTION OF LIQUID COLORS***

*Many silk painters use a hair dryer as one of their basic tools. Use it to stop the action once you see something you like. You may consider it a form of resist because it stops the movement of the colors.*

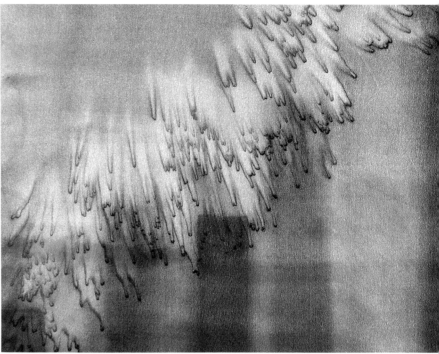

**SILK SCARF**

(Detail)

30" × 30"   Jan Janas

8mm silk, dyes, gutta, salt.

The salted background adds interest to this simple design of silhouetted butterfly shapes.

**CHRYSANTHEMUM**

(Detail)

45" × 45"   Jan Janas

8mm silk, dyes, alcohol, salt.

A 45" × 45" white silk surface can be very intimidating. To overcome this, a light wash of a color was spread with a two-inch foam brush, occasionally dipped into some of the other colors to be used in the piece. This created some light and dark areas with a certain amount of shading. A light sprinkling of table salt was used here and there. Once the background was dry or semi-dry, the design was built without the restraint of resisted shapes. If certain shapes were not too pleasing, they could easily be modified and reworked at this stage.

**STRIPED AND SALTED SILK SCARF**

11" × 48"   Diane Tuckman

8mm silk, French dyes, salt.

In this very tailored and toned-down color combination, judicious salt placement adds pizzazz. The soft gray background was washed over the entire scarf with a wide foam brush. The colors were thoroughly tested, then soft colors were striped down with a one-inch and two-inch foam brush, wet-on-wet. The scarf was restretched, then coarse salt was used, and the frame tilted to emphasize the direction the colors flowed.

Fabric used in silk painting needs to be raised above the work surface and stretched straight and taut, otherwise it will smear. This makes it easier to apply the resist and helps the colors flow evenly. Iron the fabric before stretching it on the frame if there are creases. To avoid backaches, be sure the height of the frame is correct. You can raise it with bricks or books if necessary.

## Types of Frames

There are several kinds of frames being marketed, with various ways to stretch the fabric over them. These frames are fairly costly, so be sure they fulfill your needs before you invest in them.

Most frames will work well for silk painting as long as they are large enough to accommodate the size of your fabric and raise it off the work surface. There are two types of frames: stationary (nonadjustable) and adjustable. You will probably end up using both types for different projects. After a while, you will learn what type of frame works best for you or you'll come up with clever alternatives, but here are a few suggestions.

**THE STATIONARY FRAME.** The advantage of the stationary frame is that when assembled and ready to use, you can stretch the fabric level on all four sides. You can use canvas stretcher strips, hoops or an old picture frame as a stationary frame, or you can make your own with lumber. Whatever you choose, just be sure the frame opening fits the size of the project. Canvas stretcher strips come in various sizes, so you can mix and match them. They're easy to assemble and widely available in art supply stores and craft shops.

**BUILDING YOUR OWN FRAME.** If you decide to design and build your own frame, remember that your goal is a setup that will effectively stretch your fabric. When buying lumber, be sure it is not warped — and don't get wood with knots! Choose four 1″×3″ boards of soft wood, such as pine, so the pushpins will go in easily. The length of your lumber depends on how large your project will be. You can cut slots in the wood and fit the 1″×3″ strips of lumber into them.

**HOW TO STRETCH WIDE YARDAGE.** To stretch wide fabric and yardage (approximately 45 inches wide) you will need two saw horses; two pieces of lumber (2 × 4 inches) approximately 60-inches long; two pieces of lumber (2 × 4 inches) as long as you wish,

say up to 3½ yards; two wide C-clamps and four smaller C-clamps (size: 3 inches).

Cover all four pieces of lumber with packing tape on all four sides. Place the two short pieces of lumber on the saw horses, center them, and use the two wide clamps to hold them securely in place. Place the two longer boards on top of the short ones to form the frame and use the four smaller clamps to hold the frame together at the four corners. The clamps on the four corners can be used to slide the boards up and down to stretch the fabric.

## Stretching the Fabric Over the Frame

Stretching your fabric properly is important. The fabric must be straight to eliminate distortion. *Always stretch the selvage first.* When painting yardage, if your frame is not large enough, consider breaking down the background of your design so you can move the fabric in sections as you paint.

**MATERIALS FOR SECURING YOUR FABRIC.** To secure the fabric to the frame, you can use anything from stainless steel pushpins, three-prong tacks, or long pins to a heavy-duty staple gun, or tack strips used to install wall-to-wall carpeting.

*Stainless steel pushpins.* Stainless steel pushpins with tall shanks are excellent for silk painting because they are strong, rust free, and last a long time. But they're long and tend to get in the way as you paint. If this bothers you, you can always turn the frame over and paint on the other side. When

**CANVAS STRETCHER STRIPS**

**STAINLESS STEEL PUSHPINS**

**T-PINS**

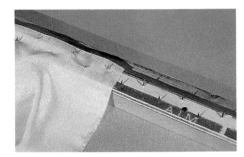

**CARPET STRIPS**

**C-CLAMPS**

*The use of strips of fabric is a good idea when your paintings are of different sizes. No need to invest in a large number of frames, just use these strips to "stretch" your frame. Actually, the width of the T-pin used gives you the added advantage of a firmer stretch.*

you're done painting, rinse the pushpins in a solution of water and alcohol to clean off the dyes so you don't dirty your next project, and air dry them before storage.

***Three-pronged tacks.*** Three-prong tacks tend to hold the fabric down well, but sometimes they rust and can snag the silk. You can lift them out with an upholstery tack remover. When using three-prong tacks or staples, follow the same directions as for the pushpins. The method applies to fixed as well as adjustable frames.

***Dressmaker pins.*** Long dressmaker pins are sometimes used to stretch pre-hemmed scarves. (See page 44.)

***Staple gun.*** Using a heavy-duty staple gun is a quick and easy way to secure fabric. Carefully remove the staples with a screwdriver when you're done.

***Carpet strips.*** Carpet installation strips are one-yard lengths of wood with small sharp nails protruding at 1/4 inch intervals. To use the carpet tacking strips, attach them to the boards on the edge closest to the inside of the frame. Screw them onto the boards, nails pointing up, and cover the whole thing with tape. Use a nailbrush (the type used to scrub your fingernails) to push the tape down over the nails. Be sure you also use this brush to push the fabric down when you stretch the fabric onto the

frame. Start stretching at the end of one board and move along the board to the other side. Keep the fabric straight. These strips are economical to buy and can be replaced frequently if necessary.

***Curtain stretchers.*** Old curtain stretchers have sharp, pointed nails protruding around the entire frame. Stretch by starting at the top left-hand corner, moving to your right, turning the frame as you go.

## Stationary Frames

When stretching fabric on a stationary frame with pushpins, cut the fabric one-half inch larger than the opening of the frame. Center the fabric over the opening and secure it with one pushpin at the top center. Pull tightly at the top right-hand corner and secure with another pushpin. Place pushpins between them, approximately one every inch. Pull tightly at the top left-hand corner and secure with a pushpin. Place pushpins between them, again approximately every inch. Pull the lower right-hand corner tightly, keeping the fabric as straight as possible, and secure with a pushpin. Place pushpins all along as described above. At this point you have one loose corner. Pull it tautly and secure it. As you begin to pin down the remaining two sides, avoid placing one pushpin directly opposite another one. When you have

*1. Center the fabric over the opening and secure it with one pushpin at the top center of the frame.*

*2. Pull tightly at the top right-hand corner of the fabric and secure with another pushpin.*

*3. Pull tightly at the top left-hand corner and secure with a pushpin. Place pushpins, one inch apart, across the top side of the frame.*

completed this step, run your hand along the fabric and push down to see that it is taut throughout. If it gives, remove some pushpins and pull very tightly to correct it. Some silk painters feel more comfortable using more pins. Do what works best for you.

## The Adjustable Frame

An adjustable frame can accommodate many different sizes of fabric and is easy to store.
**Stretching fabric over the adjustable frame.**
If you're stretching yardage using the adjustable frame, place the fabric over your shoulder so it doesn't drag on the floor. The opening should be smaller than the fabric so you can restretch the fabric after you have finished pinning it. Secure the first corner at one end of the frame with two pushpins. As you pull, move down the board and continue to secure the fabric with pushpins. Once you have completed one side, move on to the other, making sure that the starting point is directly opposite the first. All four corners should have two pushpins because these are the weak points. To pull the fabric tighter, release the two clamps on the corners of one side. Pull and tighten them. This way of stretching applies to all types of movable frames.

When you stretch fabric over movable frames, you'll find that the four sides of the frame are on two different levels and you cannot really stretch the fabric as tautly as you could with a stationary frame. Here are a few ways to alleviate this problem:

- Place an extra 2 × 4 board between the higher parallel bars and secure with the large clamps.
- Using heavy thread and a needle, you can loop the thread all along the two loose edges of the fabric and onto the frame.
- If you need to stretch yardage evenly, sew a piece of cotton twill tape along both selvages, then stretch the fabric.
- Another alternative is to use alligator clips (found at electrical supply houses). These clips are appropriately named since the clip itself resembles the biting jaws of an alligator. (You compress the back of the clip to open the jaws.) A threaded hook can be screwed into the back end of the clip, making these clips good tools for stretching fabric. First, to avoid tearing the cloth, place a piece of fabric tape on the spot where you will be attaching the clip. Clamp the alligator clip to the fabric. Insert a pushpin into the frame. Loop a rubber band or a fabric strip over the hook on the back of the clip and then onto the pushpin. Twist as many times as necessary to make the fabric taut.

5. At this point, you have one loose corner. Pull it tightly and secure it. Pin down the two remaining sides.

4. Pull the lower right-hand corner of the fabric tightly and secure with a pushpin. Place pushpins all along this side.

### STRETCHING A PRE-HEMMED SILK SCARF

*Place as few pushpins as possible directly through the hem (particularly at the corners) and into the edge of the inner perimeter of the frame. The holes do not "heal." You have good tension at the hem because you have three layers of silk. By raising the scarf off the frame, you have ready access to apply resist very carefully and completely at the critical location around the hem, if the design requires it. You will also need to paint the edge of the scarf and the hem, over and under.*

## Stretching Pre-hemmed Scarves

One method of stretching pre-hemmed scarves is to use canvas stretcher strips and pushpins. Purchase a frame that is approximately two inches larger than the scarf (for example, a 30×30-inch scarf needs a 32×32-inch frame). Using as few pins as necessary, stretch the scarf as close as you can to the inner perimeter of the frame. Always place the pushpins *through* the hem (particularly at the corners) and attach that to the edge of the frame opening. Elevate the scarf off the frame onto the shank of the pins so you can paint all around the hem, top and bottom. When you stretch the scarf, you can if you wish, wet it and restretch it, then allow it to dry. You will then have a very taut fabric that is excellent for applying resists to.

You can also use an adjustable frame made of lumber and C-clamps. This is particularly good if you are wetting your scarf a lot and need to restretch. Use very few pins. The alligator clip method can be used on the two lower levels. Use your adjustable frame and the alligator clips, being careful not to "bite" beyond the hem. You can carefully rewind the rubber bands if you need to restretch.

**ALTERNATE METHOD.** Here is another method of stretching scarves that takes longer but is also very effective. Purchase a cellulose board available at construction supply houses. The size should be two or three inches larger than the scarf you are painting. Protect the surface with plastic. *First,* tape the design underneath. Using the long, fine dressmaker's pins, place one through the hem at each corner and lift the scarf off the surface up to the top of the pins. Place a pin every one-quarter inch all around the scarf and keep stretching as you go along. If done carefully and slowly you will have a very tightly stretched scarf, easy to paint.

We don't recommend using the carpet strips or the three-prong pins for scarves because they'll make too many (and too large) holes in the fabric, which will not heal.

## Protecting the Frame

If dye becomes trapped in your frame, it may bleed onto your fabric when the stain becomes wet. To protect your frame from dye stains, cover it with tape such as packing, filament or masking tape, or paint it with melted paraffin on three sides. We prefer using packing tape because you can easily wipe it with a damp sponge. After prolonged use, the pushpins will carry the color through the tape into the frame. At this point you may want to replace the tape. Don't bother to protect the outside of the strips as they won't come in contact with the dyes.

Once you have finished painting your fabric, setting will bring out the intensity of your colors and make them permanent. Setting can be done through three methods: steam, heat or chemicals. The method you choose will depend on the type of product you have used and the manufacturer. Steam setting, for example, is only for traditional silk painting dyes. The other two methods can be used with other products and vary significantly according to the product and manufacturer. *A word of advice*: Never assume one method alone will work with all products, and before proceeding, always read the manufacturer's instructions included with your dyes or paints.

Whatever your method, you *must* set the fabric. Fabrics that have not been set are very susceptible to moisture and light and will fade. In fact, unless your environment is unusually humid, once you're done painting the fabric, store the unset fabric in a plastic bag and keep it away from light and heat until it's set.

Color-setting is an important step and must be undertaken with care, but once you try it, you will not find it difficult.

## *Steam Setting*

The basic principle of steam setting is simple: The combination of steam and heat sets the dyes, but no water can come in contact with the fabric. The fabric is suspended in such a manner that the steam circulates around it and, along with the heat, sets the dyes. After steam setting, you can wash and/or dry-clean the fabrics. Steam setting also affects the colors. So be warned! You will be dazzled by the vibrancy and luminosity of the steamed fabric. The silk painted colors "bloom" when steam set.

You don't necessarily have to do your own steam setting. Some stores that carry silk painting supplies will do steaming for a fee and are usually reliable. And in larger cities you may find commercial operations that do steaming and pleating, and will occasionally do silk or wool steaming for you. But these places are few and far between, and you are also at their mercy for quick service or damage to your fabrics. By learning how to steam set your painted fabrics yourself, you also eliminate the disadvantages of mailing your work, which cuts into your time and cost and adds the possibility of loss in transit. When you see how easily steam setting can be done at home, you will do it yourself.

**YARDAGE FOR A KIMONO**

*45" × 108" Terri Higgs*
*12mm crepe, dyes, black gutta, thickener.*

*This design was inspired by the subtle fall colors and rock shapes found in Oklahoma. After the fabric was painted, the dyes were made permanent by steam setting in a professional horizontal steamer. Now that the colors are set, the fabric will be washed, ironed and then cut and sewn into a beautiful piece of wearable art.*

**STEAM SETTING MATERIALS**

- A large pot with a tight-fitting lid or a pressure cooker to be used only for steam setting, not cooking.
- A rack or wire basket that fits in the pot.
- Absorbent wrapping material such as white newsprint, kraft paper, steaming paper, white muslin or sheeting. Don't use slick paper.
- A stove or hotplate.
- Old newspaper, black and white.
- Masking tape or string.
- Aluminum foil.
- Terry towel.

**A Word of Advice.** Never leave your steaming unattended. Choose a time for steaming when you're present. Set a timer with an alarm that will ring continuously until you turn it off—just to be safe.

Also, before you prepare your fabric for steaming, be sure the resist and the fabric are dry. Remove all excess salt and wax, if used. (See pages 69 and 79.)

**PREPARING THE FABRIC.** As soon as your painting is dry, remove it from the frame and roll it up. This will prevent creases and protect the fabric from light and moisture. You will need a clean, flat surface, large enough to work on. Lay down a piece of absorbent paper (such as white newsprint, kraft paper or steaming paper) that is approximately two inches larger on three sides than the fabric being steamed, and four inches wider on the fourth side. Don't use any type of slick paper because the steam will not penetrate, and don't use a waffled surface, such as paper towels, because it will leave the imprint on the fabric!

Lay the dry painted fabric on the paper leaving a two-inch margin of paper at the start and on both sides. Be sure that the fabric is completely flat and there are no creases. If creases are present when you roll the fabric up, they will remain after steam setting and will be very difficult, if not impossible, to remove. Don't overlap any painted surfaces because the colors might transfer. Roll the extra two inches of paper at the start over the fabric and keep rolling the fabric, not too tightly, jelly roll fashion. Try to keep the roll as straight as possible until all

the fabric is covered. Continue to roll until the entire extra four-inches of paper is used up. Close the end with tape.

The roll will usually be too big to fit in the pot, so gently shape it into a doughnut or coil it into a snail shape. You now have a packet.

In the second stage of fabric protection, lay four layers of newsprint on the table. Wrap the packet in that for extra protection. To keep it from unwinding, tape it securely or use a string or rubber bands. If your packet unwinds and touches the sides of the pot during the steaming process, it will act like a wick and draw the water into the packet and spot the fabric.

**ALTERNATE METHOD OF ROLLING FABRIC.** You can also use prewashed muslin or old sheeting instead of newsprint, a method particularly good when steaming large pieces of fabric or yardage. As you roll the fabric in the muslin, the folds are softer and you run a smaller risk of creasing the painted fabric. We prefer this method.

Place the muslin flat on the table. Position the painted fabric over that, leaving approximately five

## Rolling the Fabric with Muslin

*1. Gently bring the muslin over the painted fabric. Do not flatten it.*

*2. Note that you have left a margin all around.*

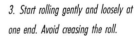

*3. Start rolling gently and loosely at one end. Avoid creasing the roll.*

*4. Gently roll or fold this into a smaller shape so it will fit into the pot without touching the sides.*

*5. Hold the packet firmly, without creasing, using rubber bands, tape or string.*

*6. It is very important to use extra layers of newsprint for extra protection.*

inches free at the start, two inches on each side, and five inches at the top. Fold the five inches at the bottom loosely and gently over the painted fabric and do not crease it. Keep folding the five inches over and over until all the painted fabric is covered. The last fold should include the five inches of muslin at the top. Bring both ends to meet at the center of the folded length and gently fold again from both directions until you have approximately a square. Do not crease. Pile six sheets of newsprint on the table. Place the packet on the six sheets and wrap it up. Tie the packet with a string or secure with masking tape.

**PREPARING THE POT.** Choose a large pot with a rack that fits inside, such as an enamel canning pot. They are quite inexpensive and easily found in hardware stores. You can also use a pressure cooker, if you wish. Again, once your pot is used for steam setting, *never* use it for food preparation.

Fill the pot with about one inch of water and place the rack inside the pot. It should be well above the waterline. If not, raise the rack by adding empty cans open on both sides. Place the rolled-up

fabric packet in the center of the rack, taking care that it does not touch the sides of the pot. You can steam more than one packet at a time.

Make sure there is adequate steam circulation and proper protection from condensation since, when the water boils, it will condense on the lid and fall back onto the packet and wet it. To prevent that, shape a piece of heavy-duty aluminum foil into a dome and place it over the roll. (Don't enclose the packet completely in aluminum foil because the steam cannot penetrate and set the dyes.) The condensation will fall on the foil and roll away to the sides. For extra protection, place a folded terry towel or several sheets of folded newspaper over the foil to catch as much moisture as possible.

Cover the pot, place it on the burner, and turn the heat on. When it starts to boil, lower the heat so the water simmers gently and continues to produce steam. Be sure there is an adequate amount of water at all times. Set the timer for one hour unless you're steaming wool or working on a piece where a lot of alcohol has been used to dilute the colors. You should then steam it for an hour and a half.

## *Preparing the Pot*

*1. One inch of water is used at the bottom of the pot, then the rack is placed over that, well above the water.*

*2. A tent of aluminum foil is shaped over the packet so the condensation can slide away. Do not enclose the packet in foil!*

*3. The packet is slipped onto the rack in the pot and the foil positioned over that.*

*4. Terry towels are used to catch condensation forming on the lid.*

*5. The lid is placed over the pot. Once the water comes to a gentle boil, the heat is lowered so that the water simmers, continuing to produce steam but not boiling.*

If you're using a pressure cooker, start the valve rocking, then lower the heat so the valve continues to rock gently. Steam for forty-five minutes. When you're ready to open the pot, lower the temperature by placing the pressure cooker under the water faucet. This will reduce the temperature quickly.

**HOW TO TELL WHEN IT'S DONE.** When the fabric is removed from the pot, it should be slightly puckered. If you dip one corner in water and the colors run out, it is not steamed properly. Incidentally, even if you painted only portions of a garment, we recommend that you steam all the pieces because there might be a very slight difference in the color of the fabric after steaming.

## Using a Professional Steamer

You don't need a professional steamer as a rule. But if you paint large quantities of scarves or yardage, you may wish to consider purchasing a steamer designed specifically for setting fabrics painted with traditional silk painting dyes. The steamer is a practical, compact piece of equipment that functions efficiently, quietly and safely.

**TYPES OF PROFESSIONAL STEAMERS.** There are two types of steamers: horizontal and vertical. The horizontal steamer is smaller and designed to set fabrics no wider than thirty-six inches. It will set approximately eighteen yards of fine silk at one time. This unit consists of the bottom tank, which holds the water, the stand, which holds the roll suspended, and the lid. A wooden rod is provided to roll the fabrics. The unit is placed over a stove with a double burner or over two hotplates. Steaming time for silk is forty-five minutes and an hour and a half for wool.

The vertical steamer is, as the name tells us, vertical (or upright) and is available in an electric or nonelectric version. The basic unit is designed to set fabrics thirty-six-inches wide, but an extension is available which will allow you to set fabrics fifty-inches wide. Approximately twenty to twenty-five yards of fine silk can be set at one time. This unit consists of a bottom receptacle, which contains the heating element and holds the water, the column that holds the roll to be steamed, the guide that centers the rolls in the column, and the lid. This steamer can easily be placed in the corner of a room. It requires a grounded 115-volt or 230-volt outlet to operate.

It is not necessary to steam silk more than an hour and a half for a full load or two and a half hours for wool, because it might yellow the fabric.

**PREPARING THE FABRIC.** The same principle for steaming with a pot applies for both types of steamers. You will have to roll the fabric first using either newsprint, kraft paper or muslin as previously described. An alternative is steaming paper (made especially for steaming), which is a practical investment when steaming large quantities of cloth, because it is wide, economical in quantity purchases, and has all the correct properties. Rolls of steaming paper are large and heavy, however, so if possible, place the roll on a table against a wall. Clamp a piece of wood at the other end to prevent the paper and rolled up fabric from falling off the table while you work.

*An additional note*: You can reuse the paper, if it's not stained, though you will need to steam the fabric an additional hour because the paper will have lost some of its absorbency. If you use muslin rather than paper, always wash it after steam setting fabric because a residue of particles of color could transfer to the next batch of fabric.

Never steam fabrics that contain wax with unwaxed painted fabrics. Iron off the wax before steaming the fabric.

Smooth out the fabrics to avoid creases. Roll them up slowly and try to keep everything as straight as possible.

When using a horizontal steamer, use the wooden dowel provided. Place the dowel on the steaming paper and cover it with the paper. You can then place the painted fabrics on the paper and keep rolling until they are all covered. It's important to keep the paper and fabric straight as you roll them. Even after the fabric is completely covered with the paper or cloth, give it an extra three or four turns of blank paper for extra protection. Then tape the entire length of the roll securely.

Use good judgment and don't make the roll too large. Remember, it must not touch the sides of the steamer. When you use a stove top steamer, as long as the fabrics don't protrude, you don't have to protect the ends of the roll. On the other hand, if you use muslin, you must protect the outside of the roll with newspaper because the fabric will absorb too much moisture.

**PREPARING THE STEAMER.** Place the horizontal steamer over two burners or two hotplates. Fill the tank with water up to the level indicated and place the stand over that. Place the roll on the stand and put the lid on. If you're using a gas stove, don't let the flame extend to the outside of the steamer because it might damage it. When the water comes to a boil, reduce the heat, but keep the water at a gentle simmer, producing steam. When steaming is complete, allow the steamer to cool down, remove the lid, remove the roll of fabric, and place it upright until you unroll it.

No dowel rod is provided with the vertical steamer, so you'll need a cardboard roll, such as one used for fabric. If your fabric is wide, you'll need two cardboard rolls. Tape them together and cut them to the correct length so they will fit snugly between the two guides inside the steamer. Place the cardboard roll on the steaming paper at the edge. Cover the cardboard roll with paper. Lay out the fabrics and start rolling. Leave a small margin of paper at both sides.

After rolling the painted fabric, place two yards of unpainted muslin on the paper and roll that up for extra protection. Again, use good judgment and don't make your roll too large. It must completely clear the sides of the column with some room to spare.

Cut off the paper and tape it down lengthwise over the entire length of the roll. Place two pieces of heavy-duty aluminum foil over the ends of the roll, extending approximately five inches over the paper, and secure each end with rubber bands or tape. Be sure the ends of the roll are open to accommodate the guides.

Place the roll inside the column and center it carefully on the guides provided. Cover the pot with the lid. Put about a gallon of hot water in the bottom part of the steamer and turn it on or place it on a heating element. Place the column of fabric over that and time the procedure from the time the steam appears through the opening in the lid. When steaming very wide fabrics you will need to use an extension to the steamer. If you use the extension, cover the hole in the lid with a small piece of fabric that has been rolled to fit to let the steam reach the top of the steamer more evenly.

## Steaming Hints for Both Steamer Styles

Never leave the steamer unattended. It's easy to forget when it's on and it could burn dry because the water will eventually evaporate. Use a timer to remind you when to turn off the unit.

After steaming, let the steamer cool, remove

When using a vertical steamer, follow the instructions to roll up the fabrics on a cardboard tube, then slip it into the column.

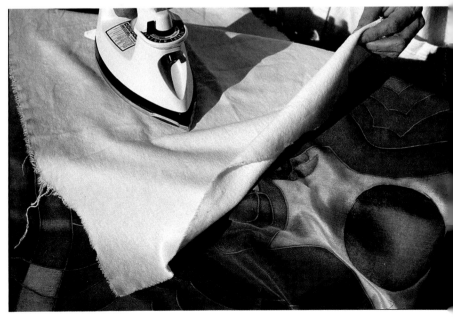

When heat setting with an iron, be sure to place a press cloth over the resin-based silk painted fabric before ironing.

the lid, and take the roll of fabric out. Leave the column of fabric upright until you're ready to unroll it.

Always dry your pots or steamers when you're finished.

It's rare, but if you get water spots after you've steamed, it's usually because your fabric was poorly protected. Don't despair—just use the fabric for a different purpose.

## Finishing the Steam Set Fabric

We highly recommend rinsing the fabrics after steam setting to eliminate excess color and the distinctive, puckered look of steamed fabric. Wait one week before washing to allow the dyes to cure. This allows the dyes to bond better with the fabric and reduces the amount of color run. But you can rinse the fabric right away in a pinch. Don't *soak* the steamed fabric, though, because the colors might run, particularly if you didn't dilute the colors enough. Some colors—turquoise, red and black, especially—are more likely to run than others.

If you have used water-soluble resist, rinse the fabric in *cold water* or very warm water as recommended by the manufacturer. To make sure all the resist has been removed, rub gently along the resist lines, particularly where heavier applications were made. It's important to remove all of the resist. If some remains on the fabric, the resist will show up as grease spots when the fabric is ironed.

When all resist is out, rinse the cloth in clean water with one or two tablespoons of white vinegar for a final rinse. Silk has an affinity for vinegar—it gives the fabric bounce.

If you've used gutta as a resist, you can rinse the fabric in cool water, but the gutta won't come out in the rinse. Gutta is removed only by dry cleaning.

After the fabric has been rinsed, place it on a terry towel and roll it up. Squeeze it gently (never wring). Heat a dry iron and set it on the wool setting. Iron lightweight fabric immediately. Heavier fabrics should be hung carefully and ironed while still quite damp. If gutta has been used, iron on the wrong side and protect your board, particularly if you've used colored gutta. Be careful not to have one area lay over another while it is wet because the colors might transfer.

## Heat-Setting Resin-Based Paints

Fabrics painted with resin-based paints can be heat-set with a dry iron. The intensity of the colors will remain the same before and after setting. You may wish to experiment with setting the resin-based dyes in a clothes dryer or with a hair dryer.

**HEAT SETTING WITH A DRY IRON.** Before you begin, be sure all water is out of the iron, since any mois-

ture will spot your fabric. Also, protect your ironing board cover with paper, muslin or old sheeting. Place the fabric to be ironed face down on the ironing board. Place another piece of paper or dry press cloth over the painted fabric and iron with temperature on the cotton setting. Use the hottest temperature that the fabric will allow. Press insistently for a couple of minutes to be sure the fabric is properly set.

When ironing silk or a synthetic fabric, use paper or press cloth for protection because the fabrics can't tolerate the higher temperature required. When ironing heavier fabrics such as cotton twill or canvas, press longer to make sure the colors are set.

**LAUNDERING INSTRUCTIONS.** After heat-setting, the fabrics are colorfast and lightfast. The fabrics can then be hand or dry-cleaned. Suitable fabrics painted with the resin-based paints can be machine washed on the gentle cycle. We don't recommend washing silk in the washing machine, but for other fabrics that can be machine washed, we recommend turning them inside out and placing them in a laundry bag before laundering. Also, avoid strong detergents.

Silks should be hand washed or dry-cleaned to remove any excess paint left in the fabric. If water-soluble resists have been used, they will also be removed by washing.

## Setting Colors with a Fixative

Some products require the application of a fixative over the painted surface to set the color. In using this method, when the fabric is dry, let it cure for forty-eight hours, then mix the fixative according to the manufacturer's directions. Pour it into a wide, flat container and immerse the fabric in the liquid fixative. Dip it in repeatedly until the entire fabric is coated evenly. Wait the time recommended by the manufacturer and remove the fabric from the fixative bath. Gently squeeze out excess liquid and rinse the fabric thoroughly in tepid water. When clean, towel dry and iron.

# 3 *Painting Techniques*

*Now that you have reached a certain level of knowledge about silk painting and the materials, it is time to discuss some of the basic silk painting techniques in greater detail. These techniques are varied and will challenge you to try them singly or combined for a wide variety of effects to create complex, exquisite works of art. Some of these techniques have been used for centuries and others are more modern.*

*In France, the term* tachisme, *which broadly means "spotting" the fabric, describes several of the techniques that take advantage of the amazing movement (capillary action) of the liquid colors on the fabrics, as well as several of the unusual characteristics of the dyes. We attempted to categorize and name these techniques, but they tend to overlap and blend!*

*Try each technique separately first, then combine two or more. Combining techniques provides a splendid opportunity to experiment. Just let your imagination run wild and try different applications of the liquid colors described in the following sections. You will be amazed at the results produced by your spontaneity.*

When a dye or liquid paint is brushed on fabric, it will spread and flow. To achieve a certain level of control over this movement, we use a "resist." This technique is very popular in silk painting because it allows the artist to interpret a specifically delineated design. Resists most commonly used in conjunction with silk painting are gutta serti (both clear and colored), water-soluble resists and wax. Look in this manual for other unusual resists used by artists, such as alcohol and syrup.

## Preparing the Resist

Before working with resists, we recommend that you read chapter 4 to familiarize yourself with the products, what they can and cannot do.

Water-soluble resists are ready to use, but before using gutta you might add a small amount of gutta solvent (one eyedropper full) to new gutta to improve its viscosity. Shake, and allow it to rest for a half hour after adding the solvent. Using eye-hand coordination, slowly pour the resist into an applicator bottle or a cone. Fill the applicator approximately three-fourths full. As you reach the stopping point, tilt the bottle back so that the resist can stop and bead. Screw the spout on carefully. Using a pushpin, make a hole in the plastic spout. If you are using a metal tip with your applicator, "thread" it by turning it insistently over the spout. Rock the tip gently to be sure that it is on securely. Using the correct size pin or needle, make sure you have a good opening before you start to apply the resist. Allow the resist to rest for a half hour so that the air bubbles

trapped in the liquid can rise to the surface, otherwise they may create breaks in your lines.

## Applying the Resist

Like all artistic endeavors, using the resist technique requires practice to apply it skillfully, in a consistent and effective manner. A peaceful atmosphere and a steady hand also help! We highly recommend that you practice applying resist on construction paper first, then on a sample strip of fabric, so that you get a good idea of how it works. Hold a folded paper towel in your other hand to rest the applicator when it's not in use.

After practicing on paper, you're ready to transfer your design to the fabric with resist. To begin, hold the applicator as you would a pencil, press the tip firmly on the fabric, and squeeze the bottle. Work with an even flowing motion, keeping your wrist loose and flexible to minimize cramping.

Use rulers and other aids to help you with straight lines and curves. Leave some room between the ruler's edge and the applicator to avoid smearing. The faster the motion, the thinner the line. Uneven lines are quite attractive, so don't always try to make perfect lines. You don't have to apply resist thickly, though heavier fabrics will require a heavier application.

Work from the top left-hand corner and downward on your fabric to avoid dragging the resist with your wrist. Place your other arm under the one you are using to steady your hand. Hold a paper towel in your other hand and wipe the tip of the applicator frequently, so threads of resist won't develop and give you fine dragging lines.

As you apply the resist, you will notice a characteristic blob at the starting and ending points. To minimize that, begin by placing the blob on the folded paper towel, then move onto the fabric. As you approach the end of a line, gradually release the pressure on the bottle. To avoid blobs, plan your starting and stopping points, and don't stop in the middle of a line.

## Hints for Using Resists

- There is a direct relationship between the tautness of your fabric and successful resist application. For the resist to be effective, it must completely engulf every fiber of the fabric on which it is placed or the dyes or paints will quickly spread beneath it.
- Resist is often used for open line work. Black resist such as black gutta serti is excellent for this purpose and is very effective when done over painted backgrounds.

**BUTTERFLIES**

(Detail)

30" × 30" Jan Janas

8mm silk, dyes, clear gutta.

*A happy color combination is offset by the black background. Notice how the resist was applied in thin and wide lines with curves, blobs and uneven detail. Occasional breaks in the lines were doubled up and cleverly disguised.*

- Black gutta serti is best applied with a metal-tipped applicator with a fine point, because the resist is rather fluid. Be sure to shake it well. It does not always penetrate evenly and you should carefully check both sides of the fabric before painting.
- Gold and silver resists are tricky to handle and have a tendency to flake. A paper cone makes the most effective applicator, because it doesn't clog easily. Shake metallic guttas very well and don't allow them to rest too long. Keep a light touch. They normally have a tendency to flake, but in heavy applications, they flake even faster. Pour in enough solvent to obtain a thin consistency and be sure that the lines are not raised.
- Metallic guttas often have a short shelf life, so don't buy them until you're ready to use them.
- Most metallic guttas can't be dry-cleaned. Check the various brands for product information.
- You can sign your work with resist before you start painting, or sign it with a fabric pen later on. We feel that it is very important for you to sign every one of your silk paintings with either a logo, initials or your name. It adds a certain cachet to your one-of-a-kind art pieces.

## Avoiding Problems with Resists

The most common problems you will encounter in silk painting involve resists. By following the general guidelines listed below, you can avoid problems before they occur.

- Follow the manufacturer's directions for use.
- Refrigerate your resists for a smoother application, particularly in warm weather.
- Don't freeze or dilute water-soluble resists. If diluted, the water-soluble resists lose their ability to contain fluid colors.
- Gutta is usually greatly improved by the addition of gutta solvent at the outset. The gutta resist should also be of the correct consistency in relation to the weight and weave of the fabric.
- Stretch the fabric tautly. It is easier to apply the resist successfully and the colors flow more evenly within a specific shape.
- If the resist touches anything below, such as a design placed too close to the fabric, it will usually smear. Be sure your applicator is in good condition. Avoid using a metal tip when working with wool fabric because it tends to snag.
- Good lighting and the color of the surface you're working on are important since they will help you see the resist better.

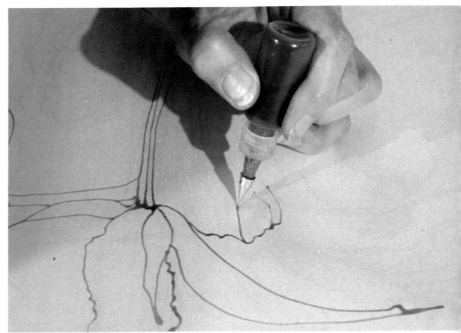

**APPLYING THE RESIST TO THE SILK**

*Study this illustration to see more clearly how to apply black resist. The metal tip affords better control and better flow.*

*Hold it like a pencil or whichever way is most comfortable. An important note — the metal tip must push down on the silk so the resist can effectively penetrate and hold the line.*

**KIMONO**

(Detail)
Jan Janas
14mm crepe de Chine, resin-based paints, black and gold water-based resists, salt.

Three yards of silk were stretched to paint a kimono. The fabric was first wet down and black water-based resist was applied over that. It tended to fuse and flow into the fabric instead of forming a crisp line. The various areas were painted with resin-based paints. Because they tend to form dark edge lines, the paints were used along with black resist to form the distinct shapes, accentuating or masking them as necessary. Salt and water-based gold resist were used strictly for highlighting.

**SILK SCARF**

(Detail)

30″ × 30″  Jan Janas

8mm silk, dyes, water-based clear resist.

Here is an example where a break in the line is so effective that it would be a crime to touch it up! The weakened lines of resist allowed the darker color to seep into the leaves, creating a very natural appearance of disease or bug damage on the leaves.

- Double-check your resist lines to be sure they're completely enclosed and then, whenever possible, hold the frame up to the light and look again. Placing the resisted fabric against a dark surface is helpful. Check for any openings you see before you start painting, and, if you feel the lines are not as solid as they might be, retrace the doubtful areas with more resist. We prefer to double up lines of resist unevenly because the unevenness makes them more artistic and interesting.

- If you think your resist lines won't hold, try the following before you start painting: Using a clean brush or cotton swab, paint the suspect area with clean water or water/alcohol solution without flooding it. If the lines of resist hold, you can safely assume that the lines will also hold the colors. Should the water or solution flow out, wait for the fabric to dry, close the breaks in the lines, and proceed.

- If the gutta is too thin or too heavy it won't work properly. So if the gutta resist does not dry in approximately ten minutes, it was not of the proper consistency or was applied too heavily.

- It's best to wait for the resist to dry somewhat before you begin painting.

Antifusants have gradually become popular because they allow you to paint in a controlled manner without having to contend with resists. Antifusants control the spread of the dyes and paints on the fabric by preventing them from moving. As a result, fine, delicate, detailed paintings can be done when the entire surface or portions of the fabric are sprayed or painted with an antifusant. On the other hand, this technique requires a completely different mind-set because the dyes and paints don't migrate on the fabric!

## How to Use an Antifusant

Stretch the fabric and spread the antifusant over it. Then let it dry. Painting on the fabric is then like painting on paper, that is, dyes and paints don't diffuse on the fabric. When the painting is complete, set the colors, remove the antifusant by washing or dry cleaning, and the fabric will return to its original, soft condition.

**USING PREPARED ANTIFUSANTS.** Some antifusants are available ready to use and others you can prepare yourself. Prepared antifusants are easy to use. Stretch the fabric on a frame. Wet a wide foam brush and squeeze out the water. Then pick up a small amount of the product on the foam brush and lightly coat the areas where you wish to use this technique, working all over the fabric, if necessary. Spread the antifusant over the fabric with even, parallel, overlapping strokes, crisscrossing them if necessary. Allow thirty minutes to dry, or use a hair dryer.

Ready-to-paint antifusants have no odor and are nontoxic. But don't use too much, just a *very* light coat. Remove the excess with a paper towel. The fabric will feel stiff, but that will disappear with washing.

After the fabric has dried, use a silk painting brush and pick up a small amount of color and paint the design. Be careful not to use too much moisture on the brush or it will break down the antifusant. Overworking the colors will also produce this result. After your painting has been set, rinse out the antifusant in water. It will disappear and the fabric will be soft again.

## Making Your Own Antifusant

You can also make your own antifusant using several different products.

● **Gutta.** You can prepare a gutta solution to produce a similar effect. Use one part gutta and seven parts gutta solvent for medium-weight fabrics. More

**CHIEF**

(Detail)

11" × 48" Jan Janas

8mm silk, dyes, antifusant.

A layer of antifusant was first painted over the entire surface. With a very light touch of the brush, the design was sketched in. Colors were delicately built up in layers to create intense depth of color along with a substantial amount of shading and detail. Note the fine detail on the feathers and the white areas scattered throughout for relief.

### SILK SCREENING WITH THICKENED DYE

*(Detail)*

*Jan Janas*

*8mm silk, French dyes, thickener.*

*It's easy to thicken the dyes and silk screen, a useful technique to produce crisp repetitive designs for yardage. Three passes were used in this design.*

### SUNFLOWERS

*15" × 15"   Jan Janas*

*8mm silk, French dyes, antifusant.*

*In this piece the entire surface was first coated with an antifusant and large spots of red, magenta and yellow were dropped on it. The artist blew through a straw to create three distinct, large sunflower shapes. Dyes were used to add stems, leaves and more details in the center of the flowers to create depth. The background was a light blue wash around only the flowers to better bring them into focus.*

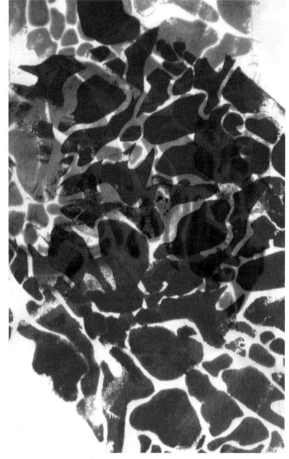

gutta is required for heavier fabrics, sometimes up to one part gutta to five parts solvent. Test for correct proportions on different fabrics and note that if the solution is too light, it will simply produce more feathering. You will obtain a sharper edge to each shape with this antifusant, but be careful—it is flammable. After setting, remove the antifusant by dry cleaning.

• **Salt.** Prepare a salt solution using one cup of water and a half pound of salt. Heat the solution to dissolve the salt. Paint or dip the entire surface of your fabric and hang to dry. When you paint over this solution without resist, there will be very little movement and you will get a fuzzy, stippled look.

• **Wax.** Wax is effective, too. Use a very light film over areas where you wish to paint without movement. Use a sharp tool and draw the design. Paint over that with a foam brush and the dye will penetrate through the cracks. You can also add a small amount of detergent with the dye and it will penetrate and coat a surface that is covered with a light film of wax.

## Experiments to Try

• Allow each color to dry on the antifusant before you use another one. Try mingling them. Nice shading details are possible. Use a hair dryer to accelerate the drying process.

• After a background has been painted, apply the antifusant before adding details in a very crisp manner. This can be done also strictly within a resisted shape.

• Try misting, stamping and stenciling using various shapes over the antifusant for an interesting look.

• After the fabric has been prepared with the antifusant, place a couple of drops of dye in one spot, guiding the color by blowing on it with a straw. Unusual shapes and lines develop and form the basis for new ideas. Use this in conjunction with misting, salted fabrics, and over painted backgrounds, set or unset.

• Some products have compatible thickeners which will also allow you to paint with a more painterly approach. Again follow the manufacturer's directions.

Because no movement of colors takes place with the antifusant technique, it is a little removed from silk painting. On the other hand, it gives you many other options for effects that would otherwise not be possible.

As you've learned in earlier chapters, silk painting has a spontaneity of its own. Even the experienced silk painter is constantly amazed at the results this medium offers. There are a variety of techniques that will deepen your exploration of color and effects to help you stretch that spontaneity to its limits. Some have been borrowed from other mediums. Some require control while others encourage abandon and free expression. Your skills and broad knowledge as an artist will help you as you learn these techniques.

## Preparing a Test Strip

Before you apply the liquid colors to the silk you will actually use for your project, use a test strip of the same fabric to help you determine your color palette. Use cotton swabs to test colors and then dispose of them.

Once you have selected the colors, apply resist to the test strip in a few shapes to accurately determine the intensity of the colors. It is necessary to use the identical fabric you will use for your finished piece because the liquid colors look different on the various weights and types of silk. Before you begin an important project, be sure to test the colors and steam set any dye sample for accuracy. Keep these samples along with your notes for your records.

To do a test strip, cut a swatch of the fabric approximately 2×9 inches, and tape it to the edge of your table on the left side (if you are right-handed) and let it hang. You can now pull it with your left hand and test with the right. It will hang and dry as you use it.

While you're applying the colors to the fabric, they will be quite bright. As they dry, however, they will appear duller. (This does not apply to the resin-based paints.) The silk dyes will become incredibly brilliant again after steam setting. With experience, you can learn to judge the final intensity. That's where the test sample comes into play. In fact, many French artists place a grid of the colors selected on one side of their painting as a reference and include it with their records.

**PAINTING TIPS.** We have pointed out various painting tips and hints throughout this book. The one we wish to emphasize again is that when you are working with a resist, it is imperative that you start painting at the center of the shape and continue to push the colors from wet to dry in the direction of the resist. You should stop and look at the move-

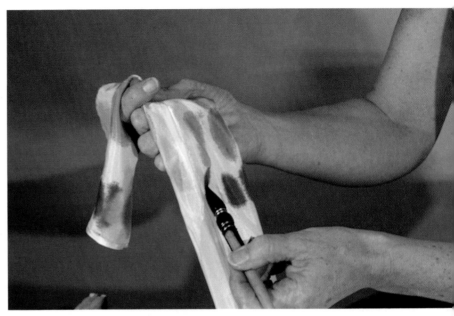

ment of the dyes and decide whether you feel the liquid will fill the space. You can then gently push in extra color if necessary.

Diluted colors require more care in painting. They streak more easily because of the water content. It is most important to overlap the brushstrokes as you paint from wet to dry, but this is alleviated by the use of the diluent instead of alcohol and by overlapping the strokes as you paint from wet to dry.

When you're painting large surfaces, the colors sometimes do not have an opportunity to even out. Using paper towels to blot up excess liquid color on the silk, and scrubbing if necessary, will correct this problem.

It's best to apply your dyes, and particularly your paints, swiftly. And stir the paints occasionally. Should your dyes develop a residue, strain them through a filter and try reheating in a double boiler. If you don't filter out the specks, you will notice them when you paint. This is even more common in the paints, so be sure you shake them very well before using and stir them occasionally.

## Watercolor Technique

Watercolor technique in silk painting is wonderful! You might consider it similar to the use of an antifusant. It is sometimes used in conjunction with wax, resist and antifusant. Soft shadowy colors appear and, with repeated applications of layered colors to the moist or wet cloth, amazing landscapes and backgrounds will develop. It is possible to interpret several phenomena of nature such as the sea, sky and landscapes in this way.

**DETERMINE YOUR PALETTE OF COLORS**

*Use a test strip to help you select good color combinations for an idea. Make sure you are using the identical fabric for a test strip.*

**PEACOCK FEATHERS**

(Detail)

30" × 30"   Jan Janas

8mm silk scarf, French dyes, permanent fabric pen.

The iridescence of peacock feathers was captured with the use of silver resist and a good color combination. The silver resist was used to define the shapes, not just as a resist. Various washes were applied in layers, unevenly, to build up deep and light areas. As the dark edge lines formed, they were used to shape the feathers. The final iridescent effect was achieved with turquoise. The brilliance of the colors illustrates how the soft feathers billow. Fine details were added with a black permanent fabric pen.

The watercolor technique requires an acute sense of what stage of wetness the fabric is in at any given time and is one of the more difficult techniques to master. When the fabric is very wet, the dyes hydroplane on its surface, with some colors producing better results than others. When colors hydroplane, they can be moved about until you are satisfied with the effect you achieve. As the moisture evaporates, you can move the colors to build and create shapes by layering. As the fabric becomes drier, look out for the dark edge lines in your colors (unless you want them). It is truly amazing how much can be done with this method of painting on silk!

**PREPARATION.** Prepare the colors you have selected at different values. Be sure you have a large container with cold clean water and a large clean brush. *Procedure.* Stretch the fabric and wet it down evenly with cold water and a polyfoam brush. Cold water will remain wet for a longer period of time. It is *imperative* to paint on an evenly wet surface; it will give you a wider margin of error. Remove the excess with a paper towel if necessary. The silk should be neither too wet nor too dry. Re-stretch the fabric if sagging makes it necessary.

Please note that the watercolor technique is more effective with the pastel shades and medium colors. It's more difficult to keep things wet and moving with darker colors. The ideal time to apply the darker shades is when there is a proper balance between wet and damp, and this varies depending upon the fabric. With experience, you'll learn to recognize the best combinations of conditions. When selecting your colors, remember the information you learned in chapter 8. Be aware of the static colors and the ones that break down as they flow. Work quickly; the important point is to have the colors *melt and blend* into each other.

Use the halo effect in conjunction with the watercolor. The diluting solution can be used to move the colors around. If at some point you reach what you consider the best possible effect, use a hair dryer to dry the fabric quickly and completely stop the movement of the colors.

Always apply the pastel shades first, leaving white areas where necessary and keeping everything wet by rewetting the whole surface when necessary, moving from wet to dry. Build the layers of color by placing darker values over the same colors and leaving the lighter shades and the white areas where you want them. Work lightly and apply the colors parsimoniously.

Should some lighter areas be overpowered by darker shades, use the 50-50 water and alcohol solution or just alcohol to move the color away. Use the brush to *melt and blend* the colors. As you build layers of color, usually from the bottom, the upper lines dry and you can "draw" landscapes, moonscapes, seascapes, etc. For more defined shapes, wax is usually used because it will adhere to the wet silk better than other resists. If you are looking for a more fluid line of resist use the water-soluble resists. Use a hair dryer to preserve patterns where you feel it is appropriate. You may even need hard edge lines to paint unusual landscapes, so don't ignore them altogether.

After the watercolor is completed, you may wish to add fine details. Use a very dry brush and proceed with an extremely light touch. Just as with other antifusant techniques, various objects, such as fan brushes, can be used to add texture. You will need to really work at this unpredictable technique to extract the most from it.

## Wet-on-Wet

This is an extension of the watercolor technique, but is worked on wetter fabric for a softer look. While the regular watercolor technique provides more control, you can get a certain amount of control in this method as you learn to estimate the drying time of your washes and see the effect of the dyes at various degrees of dryness.

**HOW IT WORKS.** The wet-on-wet technique is simple. After painting a layer of color on the fabric, while the color is still wet, come back into the wash with another color or colors to create a design. You can get this effect with several mediums as well as a wash: water/alcohol, diluent or simply water. Wherever you place the first wash, a light barrier will be created that will slow down the capillary action of the subsequent colors. The more the area dries, the more defined your lines will become, until a dark edge line appears—which you may or may not want (see page 62). Different colors also give you different effects, and only experimentation will show you which colors are the most effective for what you have in mind. As usual, static colors such as turquoise and pinks work best when you are looking for as little movement as possible. *Procedure.* Using a large, clean foam brush, paint the entire surface with a light tint of color, the water/alcohol solution, the diluting solution or water. If the fabric is too wet, wipe the excess off with

### FISH PANEL

(Detail)

A relatively dry one-inch foam brush was patted lightly and repeatedly over the painted background to create the coral fan. Note in the center the exquisite soft look that is offset by the strong coral reef shapes.

### FISH PANEL

45" × 90"  Jan Janas
Twill, French dyes, salt, misting, water-soluble resists, wax.

Quick execution was important to this successful panel. The whole background was first painted with a gradation of various colors as a wash. The shape of the coral reef and the fish were added before the background dried. Some of the fish were covered with wax and detail added later over that. Other shapes at the top of the panel were misted over using cutouts. Colored resists were used to superimpose shapes over dried areas to avoid dark edge lines.

paper towels. When the wash is applied, the fabric will sag, therefore we recommend that you re-stretch it. (This is where an adjustable frame comes in handy!)

Apply your design with additional colors while the background is still wet or damp. The superimposed colors will move very slowly and create a fluid look. You won't get any dark edge lines unless you wait too long for the initial color to dry.

It may take more time than usual for the fabric to dry, but don't be impatient. As the colors continue to move, the effect will change until the fabric is completely dry. Be aware that diluents that don't contain alcohol slow down the drying process and can affect the way this technique works.

### EXPERIMENTS TO TRY

● Paint a light wash and spread other colors in a random pattern. Sprinkle a small amount of fine salt for a discreet look here and there and allow the surface to dry. This is especially effective on shiny silks.

● Wet-on-wet salt flowers and shapes are very attractive. Paint a uniform pale to medium-light background and, using colors which are most effective with salt (see pages 68-69), organize your shapes, and apply the salt strategically for the most impact. Place two or three colors over each other for most dramatic salt effects. The blues, grays, orange browns, violets, and combinations are good. Do not oversalt with this technique—there might be too much moisture, which renders the salt ineffective.

● If you have wanted to paint plaids without resist, this is the way. Wet the fabric. Restretch tautly. Use foam brushes of the appropriate size and squeeze out the excess liquid color for the initial placement until you get a feel for the quantity needed. Stripe the chosen colors side by side vertically and then horizontally. Alternate with water/alcohol solution if you wish. After it dries, try striping with alcohol!

● Start out with a pale wash and then proceed as above. Paint an open weave plaid with the background showing. Use these open blocks for extra designs and enhancements, such as superimposi-

**FACE**

*14" × 14"  Jan Janas*
*8mm silk, French dyes, black gutta.*

*A powerful black resist was used to outline the strong facial features. Delicate areas were filled in with large brushes, light washes, and shading around the nose and eyes. The light areas in the eyes and the bold color in the lips are attractive areas of focus.*

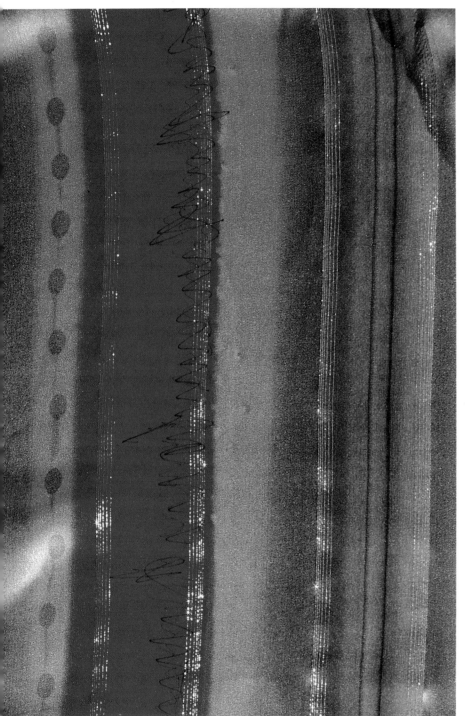

**STRIPED YARDAGE**

(Detail) Diane Tuckman

Chiffon and satin ribbon silk, French dyes.

This luxurious silk is painted very simply so as not to detract from the beauty of the fabric. The brilliant colors set off the depth of the satin stripes and the whisper of the chiffon. Alcohol over dry color, and color over color, as well as very delicate permanent black pen lines are used to discreetly customize this yardage.

tion of liquid colors when wet or dry, alcohol, dry-brush or fabric pens.

• Wet the fabric and scatter shapes with colors, leaving white spaces. Allow the movement of color to create the shapes with white areas in between. Tilt the frame for a different approach. This looks excellent when salt is used.

• For an added twist, try the following: After you have finished your piece, use a large wad of cotton to apply a light wash or water over the entire surface while still damp. Just like your brushes, wet the cotton and squeeze out the excess water before you pick up color. Use a clothespin to hold the cotton. Don't use foam brushes because they scrub too hard and hold too much moisture. This last coating has a wonderful way of unifying the work of art.

• When several colors are dropped over each other and allowed to disperse, we noticed that interesting patterns developed on the paper under our paintings. We have tried to reproduce them on silk using droppers and open this idea up for you to try.

## Dark Edge Line

Another silk painting phenomenon to exploit is the dark edge line. Basically this technique creates the unpredictable formation of hard, dark edge lines when a wet color is placed over a dry color or when a wet color is allowed to migrate toward a dry color. It is usually shunned by the average artist looking for even and "perfectly" smooth surfaces, but this hard edge line has enormous appeal! It is another one of the *tachisme* aspects of the silk painting art form that has gained greater acceptance as it has become better known and is one of the techniques for achieving maximum results with your colors. *Please note*: When using this technique with resin-based paints, allow your colors to dry *only* a few minutes before beginning. If you wait too long, the paints will have already started to cure on the fabric and will not move.

**HOW IT WORKS.** Paint the fabric with a base color. Use a medium base color for better results. But don't make it so dark that the colors worked over it appear lackluster.

Dry the fabric thoroughly after painting the base color. Now superimpose various colors over this background, one shape at a time. Put a generous amount of color on the brush. The level of moisture and your choice of colors will affect the intensity of the dark edge line. The top color draws on the one beneath, which has not been set. Note that the col-

## LANDSCAPE

*11" × 11" Jane Ihndris*
*8mm silk, resin-based paints, salt.*

In this landscape, Ihndris demonstrates
skill and timing. The choice of colors and
the finesse of the dark edge lines are
very effective. Study the one star in the
sky. This dramatic star, shaped by one
grain of salt, gives the sky great depth.
Exercise caution when using the resin-
based paints with similar techniques
because of the curing time, which is a
central element in this piece. (This is
also an easy way to stretch the silk,
paint the silk, and display the final work
all in one frame.)

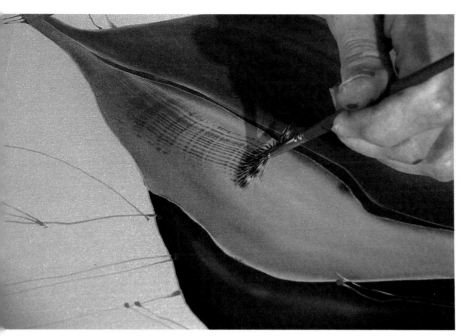

**DRY-BRUSHING**

*A fan brush creates an unusual textural effect. The brush won't hold a lot of dye or paint. Stroke off the excess and gently touch down and pick up the brush repeatedly to a grouping of finely separated brushstrokes.*

**THREE COCKATOOS**

*30" × 30"  Jan Janas*

*8mm silk, French dyes, resist.*

*This piece was executed in reverse of the usual silk painting process. A very dry brush was used to sketch the shapes of the parrots. More colors were dry-brushed on the birds with lots of white allowed to remain. The exception is the bird on the right, which was painted more heavily to move it forward.*

ors don't spread too much. This is because you are working over a previous layer of color rather than just plain fabric. You can add a third layer of color to increase the depth and darkness of the line. Of course, salt can be added to dramatize the raggedness of the dark line, too.

## Dry-brush

This technique is a variation on the alcohol technique (see chapter 16) using color instead of the alcohol. As a result, instead of bleaching color away, you are adding color, changing color, and in the case of the repelling colors, you are pushing away the one beneath. When you dry-brush, as the name implies, it is important to have a really *dry* brush. Otherwise the dark edge line will quickly appear and you will be painting "wet-on-dry." You can use dry-brushing for the design detail in a silk painting, which will add considerable charm. Another way to dry-brush is to thicken the dyes and paints for special effects.

**HOW TO DRY-BRUSH.** Using color to move paint is more challenging than using alcohol because there are several variables. Let's take a look at the process.

Apply the first color or background and allow it to dry. Using a detail brush, pick up a very small amount of another color on the tip of the brush and stroke the brush on padded paper towels to remove almost all of the color. Again, you will need a very dry brush. Using a light touch, paint a design over the initial background color. Because you have not set the color underneath, the second color draws up some of the underlying color and changes it. For example, when yellow and blue are combined, green appears. On the other hand, darker colors will usually just cover the colors beneath them.

As you experiment, you will find some colors more effective than others. You will also find that very fine details are possible when the brush is very dry. Also try applying several layers of color and see what happens.

## Blending and Double Loading

One of the most intriguing effects of painting on silk is the flow and spread of the liquid colors on the fabric. This movement, through capillary action, is particularly effective when using the techniques of blending or shading and double loading. Blending means merging several colors within a shape, a technique often used for shading areas. Double loading describes loading two or more colors on the brush or shading part of an area with a different color. As you use these techniques, a unique soft look will develop as your colors melt, merge, and mingle to create new ones. This is one way to give your silk paintings a one-of-a-kind look.

Keep in mind that colors dry and blend faster on lightweight fabrics. So if you want the same fluid look on heavier fabrics, make sure they are even wetter than thinner fabrics.

To avoid a sharp, hard edge, scrub and blend the colors where they meet. Resin-based paints may require an even swifter application and energetic blending. However, resin-based paints work particularly well on cotton shirts and sportswear, where they blend and fade out very effectively.

**ROCK FACES**
36" × 36"  Jan Janas
8mm silk, dyes, gutta.

*This design was inspired by the rock formations seen in New Mexico. The double loaded brush technique was used to capture the subtle multilayered colors of the rocks. First, the brush was loaded with two colors and then tipped with water. Very quickly the loaded brush was stroked on the silk. It was refilled often, always using water on the tip to facilitate movement of the colors for easier blending.*

**LOTUS SCREEN**

(Detail)

Jan Janas

Note the unevenness of the resist lines, which are as wide as one inch in places. The very soft melting of the colors is possible by swift and energetic blending when using the resin-based paints.

**LOTUS SCREEN**

Each panel 16″ × 60″ Jan Janas
5mm silk, resin-based paints, water-based gold resist with gold leaf overlay.

The transition from one color to the other is so subtle that it seems they melt into each other. Lines of resist were applied with thick gold gutta and then overlaid with gold leaf. The cool purple, green and blue were used to offset the very broad lines of resist. Note the different color on the background of each panel. Although the panels work well as a whole, they can be used individually with the screen folded.

## EXPERIMENTS TO TRY

- Load a brush with the lightest color of dye or paint first, followed by the medium color, then tip with the darkest one. Apply the paint with a *strong* stroking motion and watch the colors spread and blend as each color is squeezed out of the brush.

- After you paint an area with dye or paint, immediately place a small quantity of a different color here and there and allow them to melt into each other. You can also do this with water or alcohol. Avoid the static colors such as turquoise and some of the pinks.

- Superimpose colors of dye or paint while they are at different levels of dampness. Also try using different values (degrees of lightness and darkness) of colors.

- Paint a resisted area with the water/alcohol solution and immediately paint strong colors of dye within this shape, leaving some areas white. Watch the colors shift within the liquid until a very fluid look appears.

- Try placing the water/alcohol solution only partially within the shape. This can also be done with just water or just alcohol.

- For shading, use the same color of dye or paint and go over an area to gradually darken it while it is wet, or gradually add a darker color within an area to shade and shape as you paint. Shade while the fabric is at different levels of dampness. Shading is also quite effective when used with a relatively dry brush.

- Try blending without putting the fabric in a frame. Use two layers of corrugated cardboard a few inches larger than your fabric and hold the fabric down with pushpins or tape. Merge the dye or paint on the fabric in a pleasing abstract pattern. Use some colors at high intensity, dull others, and vary the values. Let the fabric dry completely before removing the pins or tape.

- Reuse a cardboard that has dye in it. This time paint with very pastel colors of dye. The fabric will pick up the colors beneath it and the pattern from the corrugated cardboard will become part of the design. To experiment with this phenomenon, stretch white fabric over the painted cardboard and tape it down. Then wet the fabric with water/alcohol solution and watch the fascinating design that develops when the silk picks up the dyes from the cardboard.

### TEXTURING WITH CORRUGATED CARDBOARD

*Try cardboard as an easy way of adding interesting texture to your fabrics. Use a variety of colors and a relatively dry brush. Place the fabric directly on the cardboard and brush the dyes on. Overlay some colors, move the fabric, and apply color again. Try this approach with heavier color application for a completely different look.*

**ABSTRACT**

14″ × 14″  Jan Janas
8mm silk, French dyes, salt.

By using salt carefully, the beauty of the colors is allowed to show through in this abstract. The double loaded brushstrokes in the background act as a nice counterpoint with an area of deep uneven colors. Color was allowed to puddle in certain areas and these were salted for dramatic effect.

When salt is combined with silk dyes or paints, the effect is unquestionably spectacular, dramatic, fascinating—and easy to achieve. In fact, many individuals are first attracted to silk painting after seeing the result of this technique. The salt technique is without a doubt the easiest and fastest with the most immediate and satisfying results— but you must be willing to accept the unpredictability inherent in using this technique.

## How Salt Works

The basic procedure of using salt is as follows: apply the dyes or paints to the fabric and while the colors are still wet, lightly sprinkle the salt on. The manner in which the salt is scattered on the fabric will partially determine the pattern.

Salt pulls the color to it, creating dark spots where the crystal is, and lighter areas around it. Salt works like this because it breaks down the components of the colors. So when, for example, salt touches violet, it may turn red in some areas and blue in others. It also discolors and lightens areas of the fabric, pulling the darker part of the color toward the salt crystals.

**HOW TO APPLY THE SALT.** Place the salt or salts you have selected in a flat dish. Pick up some with your fingers and sprinkle it with a back-and-forth motion on the desired area. With practice, this motion will help you avoid dropping it in unwanted areas. When using table salt, select a small shaker and cover all the holes but one. Try sprinkling slowly and carefully to avoid bunching the salt.

Salt can be placed around a circle, in the center of a shape, in rows, in a pattern, or just scattered. Always keep in mind that speed is of the essence and that a proper balance between the moisture and the timing is critical.

**TIPS ON HANDLING SALT.** It is difficult to predict the results with so many variables, but here are a few observations:

- Salt works better when it's dry, so if you feel that the salt you are using has picked up moisture from the air, dry it in a pan on the stove or in the oven to obtain the maximum effect.
- Keep your salt in a container with a tight-fitting lid because salt absorbs moisture readily and soggy salt will affect your results.
- Keep the painted fabric fairly moist. If it is too dry, salt won't work. If the fabric is extremely wet, the salt "drowns" and cannot react with the dyes and paints.
- Avoid using too much diluent with this technique because it tends to really slow down the reaction of the salt.
- Salt works very well with resin-based paints.
- When painting with salted fabric, use more concentrated dyes for the best effects. For salt solution painting, dissolve and filter the salt. Experiment and try applying dyes both when the salt solution is dry and when it's wet. (See chapter 13 for instructions on painting on salted fabric.)
- Salt works better on dark, intense colors or ones that have been combined or superimposed. It seems to require the drama of deep, rich, brilliant colors to show salt's wonderful effects best! So it should come as no surprise that salt works least effectively on yellow, some static turquoise colors, and some pinks.

**CONTROLLING THE RESULTS.** Unaided, salt creates a starburst or firework display or something like a moiré effect. However, you can anticipate the effect salt will have on your work by becoming familiar with the following factors:

- the type and size of the salt (more about that below);
- the amount of moisture or dryness (the wetter the area, the more spectacular the results);
- the specific color on which the salt is placed (for example, salting a dark color will create more spectacular effects than working on a light one);
- the brand of dye or paint used (experimentation is the best idea);

- the fabric and its tautness;
- the amount of humidity in the air and degree of moisture on the painted fabric;
- the different types and sizes of salts, separately or in combination, in a controlled or random approach;
- the plain unpredictability of the medium! Sometimes for no apparent reason, salt just stubbornly refuses to react with any of the dyes or paints!

**COLORS AND SALT.** As we mentioned earlier, certain colors react more effectively with salt than others: blues, browns, gray, black, burgundy, some greens, violet, Tyrian pink and iris. *A word of caution*: Avoid putting your brush in the containers of dyes and paints after it has come in contact with salt because the salt will sometimes destroy the clarity of the colors.

**TYPES OF SALT AND THEIR EFFECTS.** Experiment with different types of salt: table salt, sea salt, kosher salt, pickling salt, rock salt and special salts. The size of the grains will show different effects:

- Table salt will create a fine pinpoint delicate effect particularly if it is scattered lightly.
- Coarse sea salt forms a medium-sized round, dark spot with broader bleached lines leading away from this point.
- Kosher salt produces straighter and longer lines and gives more of a moiré effect.
- Pickling salt creates an effect somewhat between table salt and coarse sea salt and has a nice, distinctive look.
- Rock salt is more unpredictable. The size is very uneven and it often contains impurities. The effect is less delicate and it should be used with discretion after testing.
- Try other salts you may find.

**THE EFFECTS OF TOO MUCH SALT.** Each grain of salt needs an area of its own to create its special effect. If an area is too crowded by other crystals, such as when a large amount of salt is dropped into one spot, the fabric will be discolored as a mass without creating the distinctive and detailed salt effect. This is not always a disadvantage, however. You can often use this mass effect to mask an unpleasant area. Repaint the area first, then add salt. Just be aware that the salt effect will be much less pronounced.

Note that if you use a lot of salt and leave it on the fabric to dry, it will become heavy and stiff. We have never found this to be a problem, however,

because the fabric usually regains its hand (that is, its usual feel) after setting and washing.

There is yet another interesting consequence of adding salt. When fabric is painted, it usually sags. When salt is added to the fabric, it is weighted down even more and the drag lines of the salt are even more accentuated. (If, after adding salt, the fabric sags too much, you may wish to restretch it.)

If you are tempted to reuse the salt because it looks so beautiful, do the following: dry it in the oven and mix it with clean, fresh salt. The color already present in the salt will help it work a little better on colors that are usually not effective with salt, such as yellow.

Avoid using the salt technique in humid weather because the salt absorbs the liquid on the fabric as well as the humidity in the air and dries slowly, working less effectively, and becoming encrusted in the fabric.

**REMOVING THE SALT FROM THE FABRIC.** It's better not to remove the salt until the fabric is dry to get the maximum effect from the salt. There is the danger of the salt falling on a still wet area of the painting and creating undesirable spots! Still some artists prefer to remove it with stiff cardboard, such as a business card, after it has partially reacted so they can maintain a more subtle look.

Before you set the fabric, you must remove the salt. We just shake it off the fabric. *Be careful!* Salt gets into everything . . . and just where you don't want it. Be sure to carefully wipe away all the loose salt when you've finished using it. Look for it on the frame, under the frame, and in every nook and

**SALTING**

As a silk painter, you should always have on hand a variety of salts to obtain distinct effects. Realize that you can control this effect only up to a point. The salt can be sprinkled on with the fingertips or a salt shaker, placed strategically or completely haphazardly.

cranny so you won't have an accident from a stray grain of salt. It's so frustrating when that happens.

## Salt Techniques to Try

• Using a dropper, superimpose a drop each of yellow, red and blue and sprinkle some salt in the center of the shape. Then try changing the order of the colors and using different types of salt.

• Using a two-handed approach, start in one corner of your fabric and paint an area of color, place the salt on the wet fabric with the other hand. Then paint a different color next to that and place the salt with the other hand, and so forth. Keep doing this with several colors in a pleasing pattern. You can try localizing the salt in a strategic location to create areas of interest. Also, vary the size of the painted areas for interest.

• Paint different, deep, intense colors by juxtaposing and blending them and then salting in a pleasing pattern. But don't place the salt everywhere or the effect will be too busy.

• Paint yardage of uncut fabric with colors like black, gray, navy blue, etc. Place random areas of pink or red as you go along. Then strategically sprinkle salt. The use of the repelling colors is very effective in this instance. (See chapter 5 for more information.)

• After doing the above, use the following techniques to highlight and detail some of the effects: dry-brush with a different color, a pen, gold or silver gutta. You can actually create a fabric pattern in this manner.

• Outline a design with resist and then paint the design and salt the background or vice versa. This is quite effective on scarves and borders.

• Create flowers with the salt:

—Paint shapes, well spaced on white fabric, then immediately place another color in the center and sprinkle salt over that.

—Try placing a different salt very quickly on the outer perimeter for another look. The heavier salt looks best in the center and the lighter salt on the perimeter.

—Instead of separating the shapes, juxtapose them. You will see that as the shapes come quickly together they will abut each other and form unusual shapes; you can use the salt along with that phenomenon to accentuate it.

• The above technique can be applied to squares, and horizontal and vertical lines, as well as to waves. Try applying the salt where the colors meet.

• You can also use the salt as an exclusive design element on fabric yardage. Be sure to create space between the salted areas, otherwise the effect will be very muddled and uninteresting.

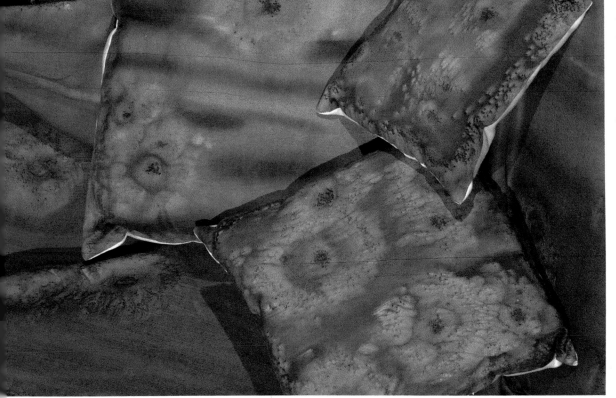

**YARDAGE AND PILLOWS**

Diane Tuckman

Cotton, resin-based paints, salt.

Tightly woven off-white cotton duck was used to paint these indestructible pillows. The fabric was prewet to allow more even merging of the colors. The circular shapes were first placed according to the size of the completed piece and then the background was blended in with different colors in stripes. The salt was placed on last and allowed to dry.

• Work wet-on-wet as follows: use a light wash to paint the entire surface, then gradually add shapes with darker colors or borders and salt the areas as you work. Then try tilting the frame so the long, bleached lines will be more distinctive.

• Note that on different fabrics you will encounter other effects. As the fabric gets heavier, the salt effect is less pronounced, but the subtle look is very elegant.

• Wet-on-dry is also fascinating. To do this, first paint the entire background with a light wash such as gray or beige. Allow that to dry completely. You can then apply areas of deep colors which will eat into the first color, creating exquisite dark edge lines. Salt one shape at a time as you work. Don't be afraid to superimpose several colors before you salt.

• Small areas of a background can be salted to relieve a completely flat look. Use the watercolor technique of maintaining the large wet area to do this effectively.

*A FINAL WORD.* Like most additives, a little salt technique goes a long way! The salt technique can be, and often is, so overdone as to be trite. We are always intrigued by what might happen, so just be discreet when you explore the possibilities, and you will be rewarded by the intricacy of what you can do with salting. You can actually use it as a basis for designing—but always with only a certain level of control. Again, this comes down to being just plain flexible.

**SILK SCARF**

*(Detail)*

*30″ × 30″ Jan Janas*

*8mm silk, dyes, gutta, salt.*

*Small areas around the orchids were lightly salted to create a textural relief in the design. The watercolor technique of maintaining large wet areas was effectively used with the salting of the background.*

Like most techniques, alcohol is used for textural effects to provide relief from surfaces that are too dark, uninteresting or flat. Alcohol can become the entire design on a blended or shaded background or much more. But it is important to note that alcohol is effective *only* with traditional silk painting dyes and does not work with the resin-based liquid paints.

## How Alcohol Works

Basically, alcohol lightens the colors in a delicate way and adds a darker edge line at the perimeter where it stops because it dries very quickly. It is a "spotting" technique. Alcohol must be used before steam setting the fabric, because once the fabric has been set this technique will not work.

You can use water in a similar manner with slightly different results. Water lightens the color, more like a bleaching effect with a soft outline, while alcohol discolors the dyes within a smaller area because it dries so quickly.

The alcohol technique works best on rich, deep colors and is great for yardage, particularly for repeat designs. Alcohol is also good for hiding problems by overpainting the area with bold strokes or by dipping the entire fabric in the alcohol to remove most of the color for a pastel look. Alcohol also renders the colors more vulnerable to light, so don't overuse this technique.

**HOW TO USE THE ALCOHOL.** Initially, use the alcohol sparingly and keep adding more if necessary. To apply, paint the alcohol in different shapes with a very fine brush for small areas or with small foam applicators or cotton swabs for larger areas. Test the effects of the alcohol on a test strip of fabric first before proceeding to your actual piece. And remember, when working on the fabric for your actual painting, proceed with caution. You can always add more alcohol to your fabric, but once it has bleached the color away, which can happen sometimes in very large spots, it is difficult to reverse the damage.

To test the effects of alcohol on fabric, dip the tip of a fine brush in a small amount of alcohol and stroke the excess off on a paper towel. Apply the alcohol lightly on a dark, intense color that has been painted and dried.

## Alcohol Techniques to Try

• Paint a piece of silk in a pleasing pattern and color combination without resist. Allow it to dry completely, then use the alcohol to draw a design or to accentuate the shapes. You can also use the alcohol to bleach out large areas of fabric for a dramatic effect.

• Within a resisted and painted area such as a flower or butterfly, use the alcohol to lighten the center of the petals, the leaves, the throat of the flower, or the wings of the butterfly. Also try using dots and horizontal strokes on the background around a resisted area for interest.

• Paint a graduated background with the darker area on the bottom. Place a drop of alcohol around the center of the piece and immediately place a touch of another color over the drop of alcohol. Repeat this in a scattered pattern to animate a design. If this is a floral, you can dry-brush a few colors over those shapes or place small touches of color to create a floral shape. Allow everything to dry, then use resist to outline stems and leaves. Those areas can then be filled in for contrast. The stems and leaves can also be created with the alcohol.

• Use the alcohol in conjunction with the repelling colors such as yellow, some turquoises, and some purple-pinks. For example, paint a dark colored background such as black or rust. Use cotton swabs dipped in alcohol as well as some of the repelling colors and dot the background, alternating both.

• Use cotton swabs to place areas of alcohol and then splatter small droplets for an interesting pattern.

• A more tricky technique is to use the alcohol as a fluid resist. Since the alcohol dries very quickly, your project will require a lot of planning and the

**ABSTRACT**

Jan Janas

8mm silk, French dyes, alcohol.

A rhythm is created by using wet over dry color, and alcohol over dry color. A quiet, simple abstract was transformed using placement of color, alcohol, repeating vertical lines, and contrasts between the solid lines and the zigzags.

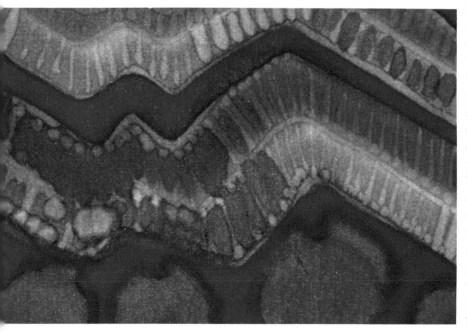

area painted should not be too large or ambitious. To proceed, spread the alcohol in one area, then paint the area next to that very quickly. The alcohol will stop the flow of the dyes somewhat like a resist would and will discolor the colors with which it comes in contact. Repeat this procedure wherever you want this effect.

● The alcohol technique is also effective for borders. Resist the border area and paint. Use the alcohol to create an interesting pattern very quickly and easily.

● Start out with a heavier fabric such as twill. Layer two or three colors for a background so that you have a deep, rich color. Use the alcohol to create shapes which become the focal point of your design. Details can then be added to these shapes as described above in the third item.

These techniques can also be done using water or diluent in a similar manner. But always be sure to do a test strip first. Unlike the alcohol, water and diluent can be used with resin-based paints.

### TESTING WITH ALCOHOL

*Test the effect of alcohol on the fabric. Dip the tip of your brush in a small amount of alcohol. Apply it lightly to a dark, intense color that has been painted and dried. Proceed with caution. You can always add more alcohol, but once it bleaches the dye away it is very difficult to reverse the process.*

### CHRYSANTHEMUMS

*(Detail)*
*45" × 45"   Jan Janas*
*8mm silk, dyes, alcohol, salt.*

*In this exquisite detail, the alcohol effect is shown off at its best!*

Now that you're familiar with the basic silk painting techniques and materials, it's time to learn some tricks that will bring your work alive and allow you to take full advantage of this medium's spontaneity.

## Misting

Misting in conjunction with silk painting is easy, fast, economical, and can be done in various ways and for different reasons. Misting is used to spray a layer of color for a background or to overlay an already painted surface. Unless you use an antifusant, misting will give you a mottled background instead of a smooth one except when you have used an airbrush.

When you place stencil cutouts or random objects on silk and mist over them, lovely shapes will emerge. You can also place these shapes over a painted background for interesting results. For more complex works, try misting multiple layers of unusual shapes and juxtapose each layer against the others.

**MISTING MATERIALS.** You can mist with:

• A plain spraying bottle, such as the one used to spray plants. It works well if you don't need an even, smooth mist.

• A mouth atomizer, which requires more skill and patience. We got dizzy from all the blowing!

• An airbrush. This produces a fine mist which is very even, but airbrushes are quite expensive and not necessary, in particular when you mist over an antifusant.

**Preparation.** Before you begin, protect your entire surface and surrounding areas with plastic and newspaper. Then stretch the fabric on a frame or lay it flat on the plastic. We personally prefer to work with the frame flat, but some artists prefer to stand the frame up. Try it both ways and see which one you like.

Fill the container with the liquid dye or paint and spray evenly with a back and forth overlapping motion. Don't spray too close to your work or you will get heavy droplets scattered throughout the fabric and run the risk of forming aureolas or halos. When misting in layers, be sure you allow each layer to dry completely before proceeding to the next. And if you use stencil cutouts, clean the cutouts carefully on both sides before you place them back on the fabric to avoid spotting.

Note that the distance between the mister and the fabric affects the depth of the colors. If the colors you select are too pale, you will have to mist for a longer period of time—and you run the risk of having heavy droplets appear.

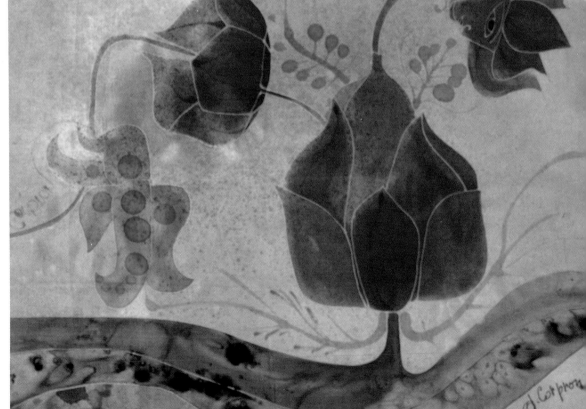

**FLORAL**

*18″ × 18″ Mme. Corpron*

*5mm silk, French dyes, resist, salt.*

*In this piece, various techniques were blended so effectively as to be unnoticed individually. Extremely fine lines of gutta (possible because of the very fine silk) were used to outline the shapes. The extra details within these shapes were added with wet color on dry color and some very fine dry-brush. The salt effect was used very sparingly at the base. The multicolored graded background was blended with diluted, subtle colors. The overall design was brought together with a fine misting of pink.*

**FISH PANEL**

(Detail)

*45" × 90"  Jan Janas*

*Twill, French dyes, resist, wax, salt.*

*Here, misting captures the underwater, veiled look of a school of fish. The positive cutouts in about ten different sizes were placed over the dry watercolor background. Three misting bottles were prepared with diluted yellow, pinkish-red and blue. To achieve the glowing look, yellow, the brightest dye, was used to delicately mist the shapes. The shapes were then moved and misted with the pinkish-red for a middle value, then moved again and misted with the blue for depth. The misting was done at a distance of approximately sixteen inches.*

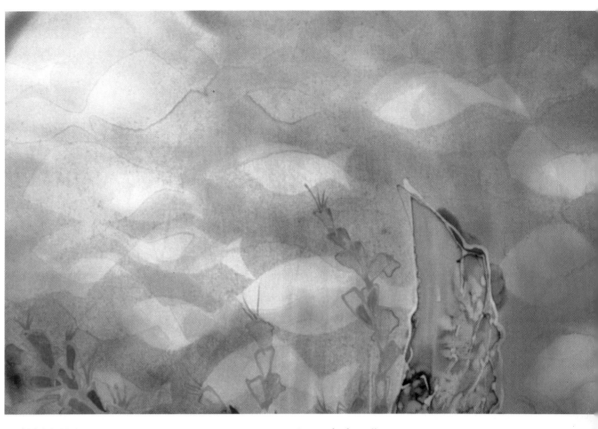

### IDEAS TO TRY

- Fashion cutouts from material such as stiff film or stencil paper. You can use both parts of your cutouts, the solid form you cut from the paper or film, and the material that surrounded it. Lay these negative and positive shapes on the fabric and spray. Textured fabrics are particularly attractive when used along with cutouts. Use weights, pins placed straight down, or tape underneath to hold the shapes down. Contact paper is also a possibility—after the shapes are cut out, peel the backing and place them gently but temporarily down on the fabric while you spray.

- Use objects such as grillwork of any type, plastic doilies, lace, wood cutouts, numbers, letters, tape of different widths, leaves and shapes from nature. Use things that will allow you to produce repetitive patterns quickly and easily, such as children's play blocks, a variety of noodle shapes, or rice scattered in a pleasing design. Do not forget to try scattering salt here and there!

- Apply an antifusant to the fabric. Allow it to dry and then spray for delicate backgrounds with dyes.

- If you are looking for darker color, wait until the first layer is dry, then spray with the same color or a darker one.

- Spray different colors in various areas, layer different objects and/or colors in a pleasing pattern.

- The scrunching technique is also wonderful and very fast with misting. Just place a scarf on plastic. Scrunch the silk into various positions and mist unevenly. Allow it to dry, reposition, and mist with a different color. After you have done that with as many colors as you wish, lay the scarf flat and mist with one unifying color.

- Subtle stripes on fabrics create a very effective pattern. There are two ways to paint stripes. The first is to mist with several colors in parallel rows repeatedly. The depth of color is achieved by the repetition. Another way to do this is to lay the fabric on a flat surface such as an acoustical ceiling board that is protected with plastic. Pin the fabric down as you pleat it evenly. Mist vertically then horizontally in even rows with rich colors. Allow this first application to dry. Fold the pleats back in the other direction and repeat the process. Remember to mist *lightly* in layers for best results.

- Select a color that is appropriate for a completed silk painting and gently spray the entire work. You will discover that the fine spray has a unifying effect which is quite pleasing. Try graduating that effect.

- Needless to say, misting is quite effective in conjunction with various techniques. Try it along with straw blowing and wax.

- One of the beauties of misting is the exquisite graduated backgrounds made possible by juxtaposing and overlaying colors. Test a number of color combinations and get a feel for the variety of effects.

- Explore the effect of misting on silks of different textures such as jacquards.

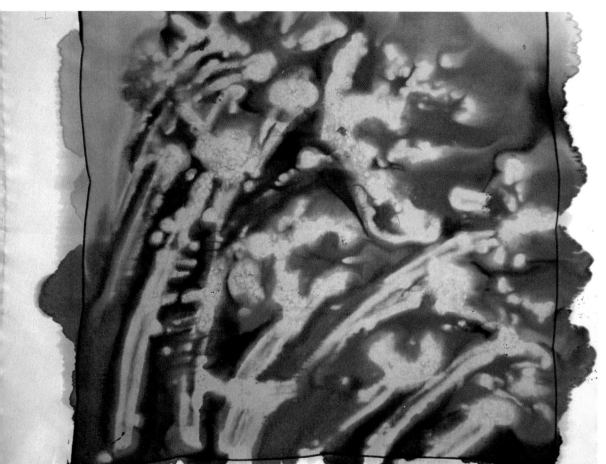

**SYRUP SAMPLE**

Jan Janas

French dyes with sugar-water syrup.

Syrup was dribbled and brushed across the silk to create flowers swaying in the wind. Colors were dropped around and on top of the syrup. During the two-day drying time, the shapes continuously moved and blended. The lightest areas indicate the heaviest concentration of syrup.

## Syrup

This unusual technique was developed in France where it is popular because it produces ethereal, dreamy effects on yardage. Make your own syrup and use this as a partial resist with unpredictable results. This technique used with the traditional silk painting dyes is very difficult to control. You may end up being delighted or very disappointed by the results, so try it more than once. The concentration of the syrup, moisture content and ambient temperature all play a role as does the fabric used, the temperature of the syrup, and the speed of application. The effects will be very soft and delicate. It takes a very long time to dry and that requires patience and space. Constant movement and changes take place even while the fabric is being steam set. Be sure you use three layers of paper when steam setting because the syrup is heavy and will penetrate the layers.

**HOW IT WORKS.** Prepare the syrup by using equal amounts of water and sugar. Boil until it has thickened and been reduced to about half its original volume. The thicker it is, the more difficult it is to apply on the fabric, but it holds the lines somewhat better as less color is drawn into the syrup. The lighter syrup will produce a softer look and the colors move more easily into it. The syrup can be applied warm or cool.

In addition to wide brushes and polyfoam brushes, try using combs, sponge shapes, brushes and stenciling brushes to apply interesting shapes. Cut pieces from foam brushes to create repetitive patterns. Protect all your working surfaces carefully and avoid overloading the design areas of your fabric with too much syrup or dyes.

After applying the syrup, paint between the shapes. You will notice that the colors are drawn into the syrup. There will be continuous shifts as the syrup dries. You can use a hair dryer, but it will still take a long time for everything to dry, sometimes up to two days. You will notice after steam setting that the fabric will look completely different from when you rolled it up. The moisture from the steam will continue to move the syrup and the colors.

This technique is also quite interesting in conjunction with antifusants, over a colored background, and with misting. It is also excellent for yardage and large areas.

## Pen Work

Working with pens is a technique that offers many possibilities. It is particularly good for bringing to life an attractive blended background, where pen lines can highlight interesting shapes or define hidden design elements. In fact, you can plan your blended colors with the idea that certain shapes will be outlined later with pens. However, the fabric must be completely dry before pens are used.

Black ink is the most popular because it has a strong graphic look. Other colors are available, however. You can also sign your work with the fabric pens.

Use fabric pens with permanent ink. Fine-tipped fabric pens are the most versatile on light and medium fabrics. Pens with a wider tip are effective on heavier silks such as crepe de Chine. Whichever you choose, be sure to test it on a fabric sample first.

Your drawing speed affects the way the ink settles on the fabric. The faster you draw, the less feathering you will experience. If the fabric has already been painted, the ink will spread less. Pen work can be done before or after setting the fabric.

**PARROTS**

(Detail)

*11″ × 48″   Jan Janas*

*8mm silk, dyes, antifusant, permanent black fabric pen.*

*In this highly detailed composition, an antifusant was applied over the entire surface. Dyes were used to paint the design. After drying, a permanent black fabric pen was used to work in the details, particularly the feather patterns.*

**TIE**

*Jan Janas*

*Shantung silk, resin-based paints, permanent black fabric pen.*

*The inspiration for this silk painted tie was a photograph by Robert Leonard. A completed, creme-colored silk tie was painted with resin-based paints and foam brushes. Water acted as a resist. Once the paint was dry, black permanent fabric pen was used freehand to reproduce the oriental silhouette effect of the photo and fill in the heavier details.*

## Painting Over Colored Fabric

Tired of always starting out with white fabric? You don't have to, you know. You can also work on colored fabric. This technique is most effective when you choose a soft color so there is less color distortion. An added bonus is that you have no white delineating line between the shapes when you use resist.

**WORKING OVER A WASH.** Of course, you can purchase colored fabric. But it might be even more interesting to paint it yourself. If you paint a wash of color over the white fabric, you can either set it or not. Whatever approach you choose will affect future results when you superimpose color over the wash.

If you steam set the dyes first, the colors that you work over will react as though the steam set color was the original color of the fabric and the lines of resist, when removed, will remain the color of the fabric after steam setting.

If you choose not to set the dyes, the second application of colors will pick up and mix with the original, lower layer of color, and pigment will migrate more heavily toward the lines of resist. This is very attractive. Again, the resist lines will be the color of the background. We recommend using gutta resist when you don't set the background first.

**COMBINING WITH PEN WORK.** You may wish to try the following: apply a wash and let it dry. Over that, apply other colors in blended free shapes. After the fabric dries again, use fabric pens to enhance the shapes that appeared.

## Batik

Batik has fascinated many generations over several continents, with its distinctive crackle effect producing beautiful fabric designs. Wax is an excellent resist, and in silk painting, you can obtain the look of wax and batik without repeated dipping. Just leave the fabric stretched on the frame and apply the dyes with a large brush after each wax application.

We will not go into great detail about wax and tools here because all this is readily available in books about batik. We are concerned only with its adaptation to silk painting. You will, however, want to look into the various types of waxes as well as more detailed information about batik.

Wax is still not too popular because of the mess, but we like it. Wax needs to be heated. The hot wax is dangerous, so exercise caution. Like many other art supplies there are hazards associated with it. Do not expose yourself to the fumes for long periods of time, ventilate your studio, and wear a vapor mask. Once the work is finished, the fabric must be ironed repeatedly to remove the wax and then dry-cleaned for the final removal of the excess. On the other hand, if used with caution, wax is quite effective and unique in its own way.

**HOW TO DO BATIK.** For the wax, use a mixture of paraffin and beeswax. For the crackle effect, use more paraffin. Place the pot on a stable surface and carefully protect the area around the pot where you are heating the wax. Melt the wax. If the fabric is heavy, the wax will need to be hotter to adequately penetrate.

Use old stiff brushes, a tjanting tool (traditional wax applicator) or tjaps (copper stamping tools) to create your designs. Apply the wax to areas you wish to remain the original color of the fabric. Without removing the fabric from the frame, use a wide foam brush and spread the first color. Repeat the wax application and then the dye application suc-

**PRECONSTRUCTED COLORED SHIRT**

Betty Ricketts

8mm pink China silk, dyes, clear, gold and black resist.

"Working on completed garments is a challenge," says Betty. "I can have a completed wearable art garment without sewing. The soft pink shade needs to be taken into account when the colors are selected. Where the clear resist is used, the outline reverts to pink when the resist is removed. Note that I took advantage of the extra surface on the back and repeated part of the design there also."

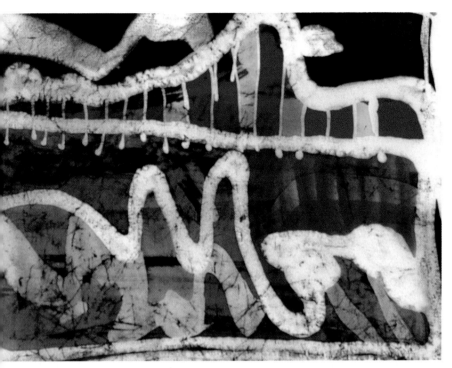

## ABSTRACT

*8" × 8"  Jan Janas*

*8mm silk, dyes, wax.*

*The fabric was stretched and the elements of the design were applied with a tjanting and a bristle brush. Shapes were painted with a watercolor-type brush within the waxed areas using different colors and blending. All painted areas were covered with wax. The fabric was removed from the stretcher, crackled, restretched, and a coat of black dye was brushed over the entire surface with a two-inch foam brush to bring out the distinctive crackle effect.*

cessively in layers. Be sure that the fabric is dry before applying the wax and never use a hair dryer to hasten the process, because it would melt the wax! Carefully remove the droplets of dye which remain on the wax because they will transfer and cause problems down the road.

To obtain the crackle effect, remove the fabric from the frame after the last application of wax. Refrigerate the fabric for the best crackle effect. Gently crumple the fabric at random or in specific patterns and folds. Restretch the fabric. Paint the final coat of color, which is the darkest, over the entire surface. The distinctive traditional batik look will appear. You may wish to try using alcohol instead of a dark color for an unusual, soft look.

When the work is finished, place it between layers of newspaper and iron the wax out, repeatedly replacing the paper if necessary. You can then set the dyes or paints. The last fine film of wax can be removed by dry cleaning.

Wax has an immediacy to its application—it flows quickly and you need to move fast. This trait, plus its crisp lines, make it quite intriguing for the creative artist.

## Stamping

Stamping offers interesting possibilities for repeat patterns and intricate designs. Basically, a stamp is used to obtain a repeating design motif. It can easily be done in various ways. Resist, dyes and paints can be used for stamping.

### MATERIALS

*Stamps.* Rubber stamps are the most commonly used. They are available everywhere, ready to use with different designs and shapes. Other objects are also effective such as tjaps (Indonesian copper stamps), linoleum cuts, art gum erasers (cut with an X-Acto knife), sponges, foam brushes that have been cut and scored, plastic peanut packing, or anything that will create a print.

*Dyes and paints.* The traditional silk painting dyes flow more easily on the fabrics and will therefore need to be thickened for best results. The resin-based fabric paints are somewhat more static and forgiving. They can also be thickened if you find it necessary.

*Stamp pads.* Use blank cloth stamp pads, special foam pads for stamping, or simply use a piece of sponge or foam rubber placed on a dish.

### HOW TO PROCEED

*Resists.* Dip the stamp into the resist. Stamp it once on a piece of scrap fabric to remove the excess resist from the stamp before placing it on your work. Do this every time you dip the stamp in the resist. Test this thoroughly before proceeding. Stamping is very effective when done with wax and the tjap.

*Dyes.* When using dyes on lightweight fabrics you will need to thicken them with the appropriate product. How much you thicken the dye will vary with the rate at which the fabric absorbs the dyes. We particularly like this technique with textured fabrics such as noil, shantung and silk broadcloth. Again, we recommend prestamping on a sample swatch every time you dip the stamp in the dye. You can also brush the thickened dyes onto the stamp itself before applying.

*Paints.* With the resin-based paints, you will notice that they set up faster, and it is easier to work with this technique using less thickener. Again, it is important to prestamp once on your sample swatch before you stamp on your project.

Use a cushioned surface such as a pile of newsprint or an old blanket with a top protective cover. The fabric has more give and lighter fabric can then be used more effectively.

Stamping can be done on plain white or lightly colored fabrics. Try using fabrics which have been treated with antifusant. Extra details can be stamped onto completed silk paintings.

A few years ago I [Diane Tuckman] was in contact with an artist who created the most exquisitely detailed and sophisticated silk paintings using the traditional silk dyes, a rubber stamp (only one shape), and a few colors on silk shantung. If memory serves me right, she placed the fabric on a padded table, saturated ink pads with the dyes and stamped the fabric. By cleverly placing the colors and using a triangle as her shape, she designed and executed large wall hangings. The visual effect was spectacular . . . the color placement created a dramatic changing pattern.

Explore the possibilities and you will be delighted with the results.

## Free-Form Ideas

**SCRUNCHING.** If you are intrigued with the idea of painting without stretching the fabric, you will definitely want to try this. We have found it to be most effective if you prewet the fabric. You then scrunch the fabric and make hills and valleys. With a dropper or large brush, apply one color of dyes or paints generously but randomly. You can move the fabric and continue to apply various colors or you can leave it as is and only change color. Try placing the wet fabric over textured surfaces such as corrugated cardboard or plastic bubble packaging material of various sizes and shapes. A pattern will develop which will open up new ideas for shape enhancement. This is quick, easy and fun. Dry the fabric, then rinse out the excess dyes before setting. Surprisingly, it works because you have saturated the fabric so much.

**FOLD AND DIP.** This is a variation on tie-dye which is, of course, also a possibility. Fold a long strip of fabric or a scarf in whatever pattern you prefer until you have a small square or oblong. (Try this out with paper first to determine the correct way to fold so you have even spacing of the colors.) Prepare a small quantity of two compatible colors in wide-mouthed containers. Dip one side of the fabric into the first color until all the dye is absorbed. There should be white left on the opposite side. Flip the fabric around and dip the other side into the second color. Unfold, and presto! you have lovely tie-dyed fabric. Experiment with the folds, color combinations and maybe some true tie-dye. Use rubber bands, twine, knots, clamps, clothespins and basting stitches. Try prewetting the fabric or not. Use ideas in tie-dye books and take it from there. You could also combine the scrunching and salt technique along with fold and dip.

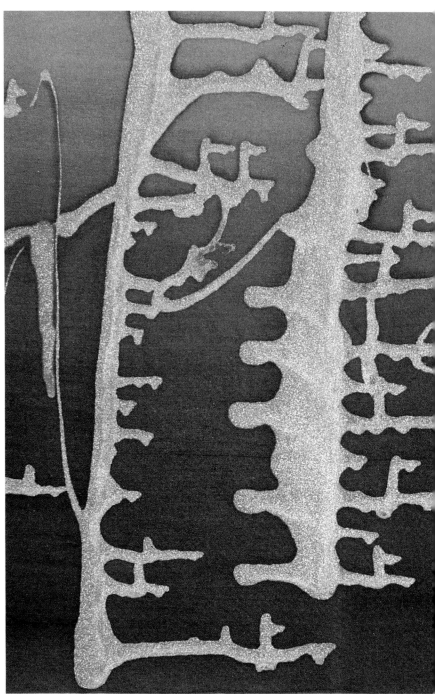

**BURNT FOREST**
20" × 20"  Jan Janas
5mm silk, dyes, silver gutta.

The tilt and run effect is dramatically achieved with thinned silver gutta resist. The very fine silk allows the thinned resist to move easily and quickly to create this abstract design. Use quick wrist movements to tilt the frame in various directions before the resist can set. The subtle gradation of color sets off the cooler effect of silver resist.

**MULTIPLE LAYERS.** It is possible to paint multiple layers at one time, but only with lightweight fabrics. One way is to stitch the edges carefully together, stretch the layers very tautly on a frame, and paint free-form designs. After they dry, the designs will be similar. This is also effective on a padded surface where all the layers are pinned down tightly and the quantity of the liquid is carefully controlled.

**TILT AND RUN.** With this technique, the frame is tilted to allow free movement of dyes, paints and resists so the designs can take shape. Using a hair dryer is sometimes effective if you wish the colors or the resists to dry quickly. The spontaneity of this technique is magical!

● *Antifusant.* Pretreat the fabric, which is either white or painted, with an antifusant. After it dries, place dyes or paints on the fabric in spots or lines with a dropper. Then tilt the frame in various directions, working rapidly since the colors *run* very quickly on the surface. Because the fabric has been treated, you can easily work one color or shape at a time. Protect your working surface and watch carefully what is taking place so you can adjust your movements.

● *Guttas.* Use thinned, clear, black, colored or metallic guttas and resists. Tilt the frame, apply the resist, and let it run. Stop and change direction occasionally. After the resist dries, you can place colors between the shapes or apply a gradation of colors over the entire surface.

● *Tilting the frame.* Using foam brushes, place dyes or paints generously at the top of the frame and allow them to drip. Use lights and darks as well as the diluent to obtain contrasts. Change direction and do this again while the first colors are still wet or wait until they dry if you wish.

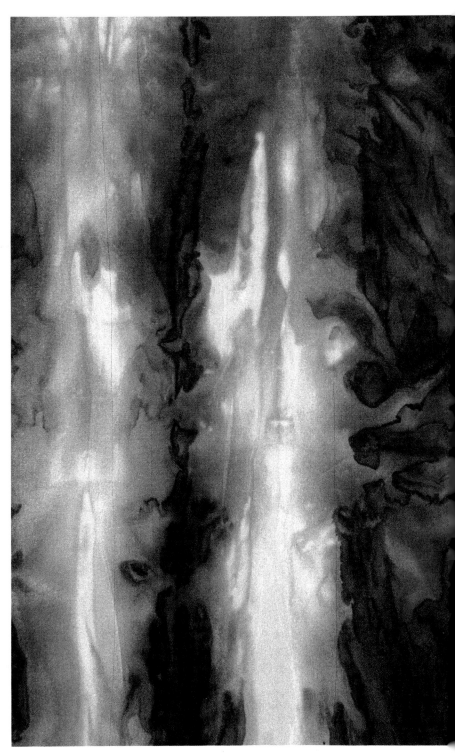

**ABSTRACT SCRUNCH SILK SCARF**
15" × 54"  Jan Janas
8mm silk, dyes.

First, heavy plastic was placed on the floor with the wet fabric on top. The silk was folded, pleated, and held in place with clothespins to create a pattern. Droppers were used to place color along the length of the scarf. Some light and dark colors were used and allowed to puddle and mix in the folds.

### APPARITION

*60" × 84"*

*Twill and organza, French dyes.*

"A bottom layer of 12mm twill is handpainted and adorned with some extra relief of crumpled organza sewn on top. A top layer of handpainted cutout organza is placed on that, without being sewn or glued to the background, like a veil hanging in front of another picture. Each of these two layers has its own composition. The addition of these two compositions viewed in transparency adds to the playfulness and surrealism of the composition. All of my works are designed to hang as art pieces."
—Marie-Laure Ilie, California

# Silk Painting with the Pros

Here we present a gallery of works by talented silk painting artists from Europe and North America. We suggest you use this gallery to study the range of work possible in the medium of silk painting, to see the way some of the techniques discussed in this book were used, and to get ideas ("visual pointers from the pros") you may be able to apply to your own work.

We looked for works that illustrated specific techniques as well as unusual interpretations of silk painting to present you, our readers, with a broad range of applications possible in this medium. Limitations of space, of course, forced us to eliminate many wonderful works of art.

Several of the artists in this gallery have exhibited their work in museums and galleries, and we hope this book will inspire museums to mount future exhibitions of this unusual and exciting art form.

### GARDEN FLOWERS

*42" × 42"*

*Crepe de Chine, gutta resist, French dyes and wash technique.*

*"My work is a refreshing contrast to the bombardment of a highly technical, slickly mechanical consumer society. It is highly touchable and delicate. The subject matter is of an organic nature. There is a fascinating pleasure in working on such lustrous fibers formed from little cocoons."*
*— Leslie Rogers, New York*

### TIDE WANING

*36" × 40"*

*Crepe de Chine, gutta resist, French dyes and wash technique.*
*Leslie Rogers*

## HANGED MAN

French dyes, salt, wet blends and mixed media consisting of fabric paints and oil pastels.

"While I work primarily with acrylic on canvas, silk painting provides me with an additional creative outlet that incorporates the fluidity and spontaneity of watercolor and satisfies my urge to work with fabrics."
— Devereaux Chivington, Georgia

**FABRIC DETAIL**

*Silk satin, gutta resist, French dyes and*
*color overlay technique.*
*Hilary Gifford*

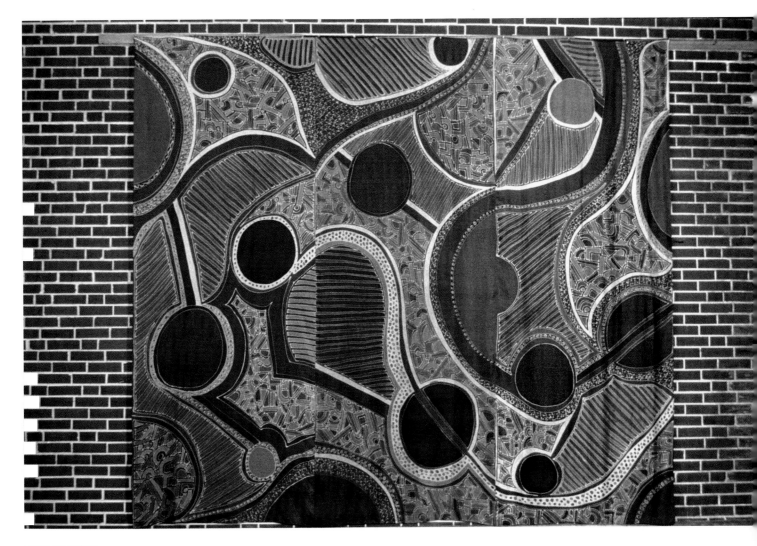

## WALL HANGING

*Silk shantung, gutta resist, French dyes and color overlay technique.*

*Beginning with a handpainted piece, Gifford extracts and reworks the design elements, either separately or in combination. Each pattern has its unique character, and by adding or deleting simple elements, the tone of the piece may change. A love of change and the desire to experiment are what inspire Gifford to continually create. "There is always a discovery, something new, different . . . untried possibilities."*
*— Hilary Gifford, Massachusetts.*

**LA DANSEUSE AUX SERPENTS**

Gutta resist on 8mm habutai China silk.

"I love working on silk and although mine is a tedious process before I even get to the dyes, it is a wonderful challenge. The colors are truly luminous, and I am always trying to get more intricate patterns and shapes for my border designs. I hope my paintings reflect the fun I am having with this art. I thank my daughter Elizabeth for introducing me to silk painting and encouraging me to pursue it. A watercolorist would be in shock watching me work on silk!"

—Jan Ryan, South Carolina

### JAZZ

An adaptation of Henri Matisse
illustration from the book Jazz.
Wall hanging or scarf.
French dyes and resist.

"I was first introduced to silk painting
about six years ago. While at a trade
show in Chicago, I whipped by Diane
Tuckman and her booth, stopped cold in
my footsteps, made a U-turn and was
immediately mesmerized and hooked for
life (on silk painting). Although I am a
professionally employed artist, my desire
is to someday completely dedicate
myself to pushing silk painting to its
limits. The possibilities and variety that
silk painting offers are boundless. The
intensity, the vibrato and crisp clarity of
the French colors makes this the most
exciting medium I have ever used. I
encourage all artists to try it."
— Sharon A. Blake, Michigan

**GOSSAMER GOWN AND
SHAWL**

*Layering of colors in free-form
techniques.*
*Sandra Rubel*

### PLEATED ENSEMBLE

*Silk and French dyes in free-form
application.*

"I am an artist first and foremost. I am attracted to silk painting because of the way it allows me to capture light, color and texture. Silk is the ideal format because it attracts "light" to color and holds it in a unique way. It drapes well on the body and brings "light" to the person. The feel and the transparency give it still another dimension. I find movement of the silk and the dyes very exciting and the surface dictates how I work. I always work outside in large spaces such as Big Sur. The elements participate in my work such as grass, rain, rocks, etc. I start very light and layer the colors up to sixty times using the free movement of the dyes."
—Sandra Rubel, New York

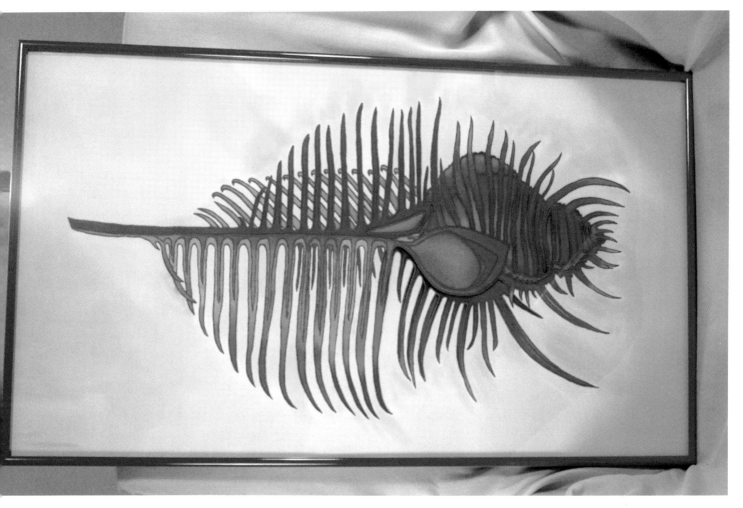

**VENUS COMB MUREX
SEASHELL**

*Silk, French dyes and red gutta.*

*"Silk painting is my form of relaxation,
fun and some profit! I enjoy the artistic
challenges it offers."*
*—Angela Marie Woodruff, Texas*

## BARREAUX DE SEL

5mm China silk, French dyes, color over color, and salt.

"The technique I most prefer is watercolor on silk for which I often use wax. Silk painting is, for me, a conversation between the fabric, the student, and me, as we create with joy and enthusiasm."
—Litza Bain, Paris, France

## SCARVES

French dyes, 8mm China silk and resist technique.

"I was introduced to this medium through a chance meeting with a silk painter. I immediately fell in love with it. The thing I like about silk painting is that you can be totally free with regard to the subject. As a painter I became known for painting women and children. I now feel free to pursue diverse subjects such as a portrait of Nefertiti, a rushing waterfall, a single iris blossom or purely abstract designs. I have no problem with the debate over the relative value of art versus craft, or where silk painting fits in. Picasso also made pottery and there is no reason why I cannot paint silk scarves."
—Constance Byrd, New York

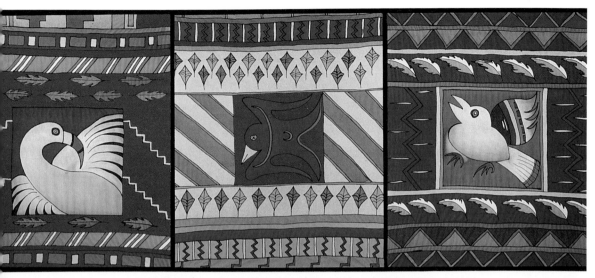

**AZTEC BIRDS**

Three panels of silk pongee with black gutta resist and French fabric paints, heat-set.
Carol Racklin-Siegel

**LANDSCAPE TRYPTIC**

Silk pongee, black gutta resist, French fabric paints and salt technique.
Carol Racklin-Siegel

**JAPANESE LANDSCAPE TRYPTIC**

Silk pongee with black gutta resist and French fabric paints.

"My personal evolution toward direct painting on fabric started with a fascination with batik. I am most intrigued with creating watercolor gradations on fabric and the ease with which the French dyes and paints flow allows me to create in a very satisfying way. I enjoy the graphic control, reaction of different substances, and experimenting to obtain surprise results."
— Carol Racklin-Siegel, California

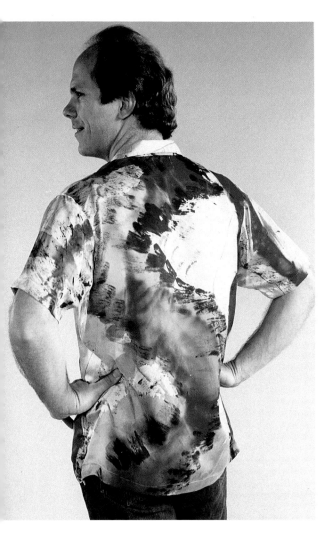

### MAN'S SHIRT

Free-form style "celebration" on silk with French dyes and metallic fabric paints.

Claudia MacGruer, New York

### GEOMETRIC WALL HANGING

12mm China silk, French dyes and gutta resist.

"When painting on silk, I particularly enjoy working with geometric and arabesque motifs in the tradition of Islamic art. As in my work with ceramic tiles, I have precise control of patterns and colors, but also the gratification of seeing immediate results in a more fluid medium."

—Dominique Bello, Washington, D.C.; Cairo, Egypt

## SILK PATCHWORK JACKET

French dyes, gutta resist, wax and various techniques.

"Different weights and weaves of silk were painted with gutta resist and wax, or had color applied directly to the fabric. Each patch of silk was hand stitched to a wool base and then embroidered around each patch. Sometimes I use wood block stamps with wax or pigments, or a sponge, or brushy watercolor effects to create different textures. Because the possibilities for designing on silk using the French dyes are almost endless, and the resulting colors are so beautiful, creating these designs is not only a joy for me but also welcomed by the textile industry. My original designs are sold commercially and printed on all sorts of fabrics for women's wear."
— Christa VanValkenburg, Pennsylvania

## KIMONO

French dyes and fabric paints on silk Charmeuse, overpainted with stencil, sponge and brush.

"I find silk painting challenging in producing costumes for Broadway, the circus, opera, dance, TV and film. I use a wide variety of techniques and products on fabrics, from silk to synthetics. I am often challenged to find ways of producing a certain look for a designer within limited time and budgets."
— Joni Johns, New York

**RICKY HENDERSON**

*Courtesy of the National Baseball Hall of Fame and Museum, Cooperstown, New York.*
*French dyes on silk, monochromatic color scheme.*

*"For many years I worked in soft sculpture, but I wanted more detail in my work. Painting seemed to interest me, and having dyes, gutta and silk, I thought I'd try painting on silk. Wanting a dramatic subject, I concentrated on sports. The main attraction of silk painting is the surface quality it imparts. Somehow the combination of dyes on silk suggests life and vitality — qualities that are missing in any other type of painting that I've ever tried. This characteristic enhances my paintings and gives them a life of their own."*
—Shar Tikkanen, Toronto, Canada

## VASE OF FLOWERS

*35" × 26½"*

*10mm silk habutai, gutta resist, and procion liquid-reactive dyes.*

"Silk painting for me initially was an extension of watercolor painting. I found the silk so receptive and the colors so vibrant that I no longer work on paper. I also saw silk painting as a way to wear art and not to just frame it, but to see it move as sculpture as it drapes the human body and flutters with movement. The resist, for me, is a drawing technique. The lines form the basis for the application of color, which gives it dimension and perspective. I paint on silk every day and it never ceases to fill me with awe and wonder as well as the insatiable desire to see what will happen next."

— Linda Prenger, Missouri

**WHALE WATCH**

Silk crepe de Chine, French dyes and
some salt technique.

"I first got the wonderful inspiration to
work in silk from a silk painting class.
I am always amused by the fact that
this medium cannot be properly
"placed" and I am forced to press on
for innovation as we show our work."
—Jennifer Cauffman, Pennsylvania

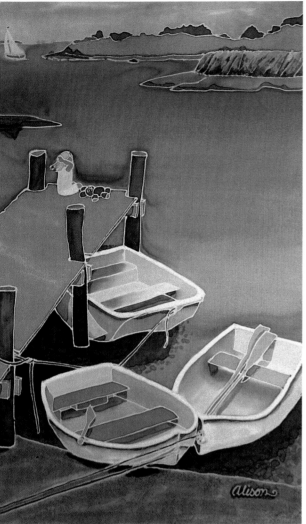

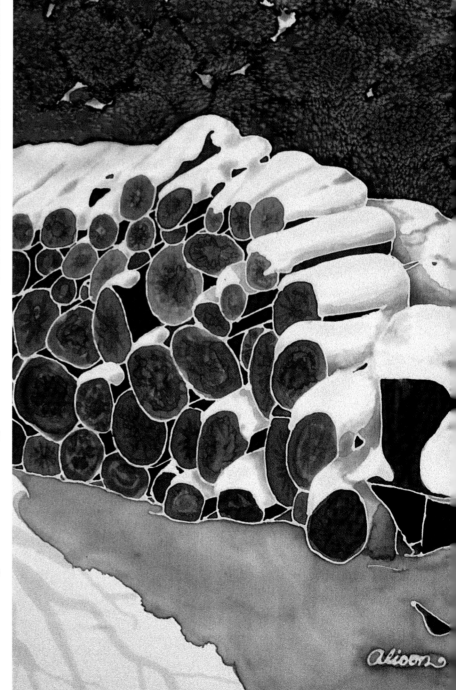

**BOATS AT MENEMSHA**

*French silk dyes, 8mm China silk, gutta*
*resist and salt technique.*
*Alison Gray*

**WINTER LOGS**

*French silk dyes, 8mm China silk, with*
*resist and salt techniques.*

*"I discovered silk painting while on*
*vacation. Most of all I respond to the*
*outlining aspect of silk painting, even*
*more than to the luminous colors*
*whether primary or muted. The hazards*
*of sneezing, wrong color choices, and*
*"bleeds" make for a perilous and*
*exciting art form. As a teacher, I look*
*forward to introducing this art form to*
*my students some day."*

*—Alison Gray, Connecticut*

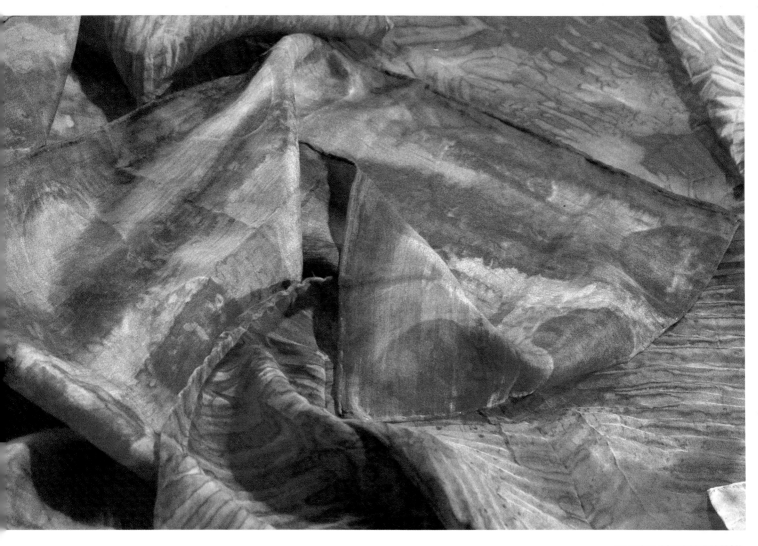

**SHIBORI SCARF VARIATION**

10mm China silk, French dyes.
Fabric was folded and clamped, dye
discharged. The fabric was then
overdyed while folded and clamped.

"I was forced to silk paint after I
accepted a commission that required the
use of the silk painting techniques. I
find the transparent quality of the French
dyes most appealing because of the way
I work. I often paint a layer, steam set,
and repaint repeatedly. I also like the
watercolor quality and hard edges of the
dyes. The dyes also work well on my
triaxial weavings of silk and wool."
—Mary Klotz, Maryland

**FRAGMENTARY ALLIANCE—
JACKET**

*19mm silk Charmeuse, French dyes.
Handpainted fabric strips, serged,
pieced, and appliquéd.
Sharon Adee*

**SCARF**

*19mm silk Charmeuse, wax and French
dyes.*

"Silk, the luxuriant, exotic fabric of
ancient times, evokes images of past
opulence. This expressive fiber is my
medium of choice. As a fine artist I
selected silk Charmeuse because of its
luminescence and soft drape. I use layers
to create subtle blends to heighten the
radiance of the silk. I enjoy creating
fabric works of art suited to persons who
dress dramatically and uniquely."
— *Sharon Adee, Oklahoma*

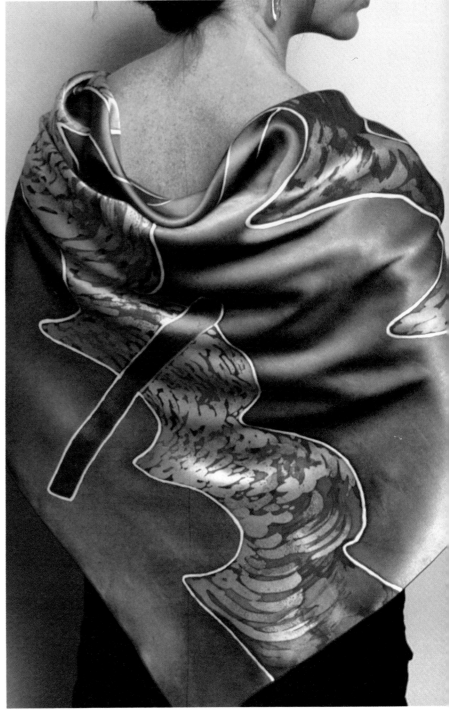

### JACKET

Silk jacquard, French dyes and French fabric paints, free-form techniques.

"I have painted with oils and watercolors all my life. The transition to painting on silk was a natural progression. It was a new and exciting experience to discover the intricacies of the reactions with the many varieties of silk, so different from canvas, which always reacts the same. I learned through persistence and experimentation and the result was constantly satisfying and new, and continues to be so."
—Phyllis McLean, New York

### SILKSCAPES: GAUGUIN, SCARF AND PURSE

14mm crepe de Chine, black resist and French dyes.

"Working from different directions in textile art, we were intrigued with silk painting. Diane Tuckman introduced us to the art form and we decided to tackle a project together and from there the business took off. Lynn moved to the Philippines and our business continued long-distance. Lynn established a studio and trained local, experienced batik craftsmen to silk paint. We continue to produce a collection there five times a year and the demand constantly grows. We like working with the finest material—silk—and we enjoy the constant challenge of designing. We like the humorous and conversational pieces we design. Our greatest joy is when our designs and color combinations bring a smile to individuals who see our work."
—Alison Abbott, Massachusetts and
—Lynn Weinberg, Georgia

**TUNIC TOP**

French dyes and water-soluble resist on silk.
Earllene Dakan-Weiss

**WALL HANGING**

Combination of batik, wax resist and handpainting on silk.

"My creative thrust with silk painting has been abstract expressionism. I love flat surfaces (scarves, ties, upholstery fabric and wall hangings), but art clothing is my most satisfying form of expression."
— Earllene Dakan-Weiss, California

**CARROT-TOP MEETS THE ANNELID**
Batik and direct painting with French dyes on silk.
W. Logan Fry

**PISCINE TRANSFORMATION**
(Detail)
Plain weave, silk warp painted with French dyes.

"My work represents an attempt to bring color, imagery and narrative to woven fabric. To accomplish this, I have chosen to work with traditional fibers and textile techniques to produce fabrics which may be displayed on the wall or used in garments and home furnishings. Each of my pieces suggests alternative stories.

They have a personal meaning, of course, but I have not attempted to impose my own point of view on the work. Viewers are encouraged to formulate their own scenarios and conclusions. It seems to me that this is one of the defining elements of art: the quality of engaging in a dialogue with a diversity of people — different ages, backgrounds and education — who bring their own experience and understanding to the process."
— W. Logan Fry, Ohio

## SUMMER ROSES

*French dyes, watercolor technique and
resist on silk.*

*"Originally from Buenos Aires,
Argentina, I discovered silk painting
while in London in 1984. I immediately
knew that I had to learn this art form.
I took my first class from a German
teacher and I have since taken several
courses. I now teach silk painting in
Norway, Sweden, Finland and India.
I also manufacture garments and
accessories and import the products.
I use all the various silk painting
techniques plus a few that I developed
myself. I am still thrilled by silk painting
and feel that every day I learn something new and fascinating. To paint on
silk makes me happy."*

*—Maria Malmberg, Eidanger, Norway*

**BUTTERFLIES**

Framed painting, 14mm twill, French dyes, with silver and black resist. Andree Borremans is an interior designer who uses silk painting in her work. Andree Borremans, Bruxelles, Belgium

**ORCHIDS**

Decorative panel, 14mm twill, French dyes, black and silver gutta.
Andree Borremans

**BIRD**

Framed painting, crepe de Chine, traditional gutta serti with watercolor background, French dyes.
Andree Borremans

## LILITH

9mm China silk, gutta resist and
French dyes.

"When I first discovered silk painting in
1976, my first attempts were very crude.
A young man introduced me to the art
of silk painting and I quickly developed
a love affair with silk. After enrolling in
a drawing class, I developed my style.
A thousand and one nights and
mythology are my inspiration and I am
always transported into history and the
relationships between men and women.
I now devote full time to my art."
—Anne-Lan, Paris, France

**FAMILY TREE**

Pieced painted silks, silk dyes and resist.
Shirley T. Waxman

**CHALLAH COVER AND WALL HANGING**

Silk dyes and resist.

An accomplished needlewoman, Shirley Waxman turns unfinished silk and other exotic fabrics into decorative pieces of wearable and functional Judaic ceremonial objects. Her themes are based on ethnic folklore and are painted with silk dyes and often pieced.
Shirley T. Waxman, Maryland

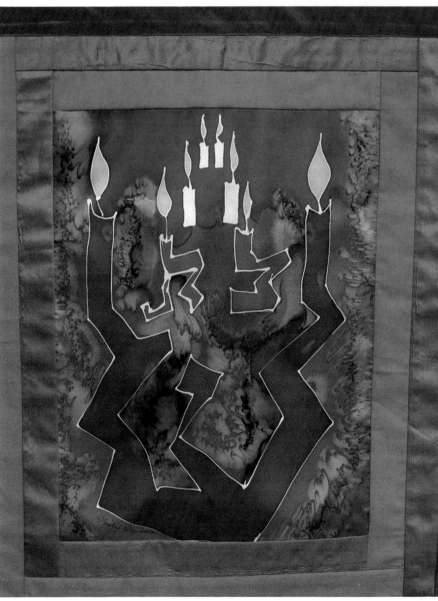

## PERSONNAGES NAIF

*French dyes, gutta serti on silk satin.*
*Sample textile design for printing.*
*Florence Niasse*

### DESIGN AND PUZZLE

*Satin crepe, French dyes, several pieced and quilted silks, crepe de Chine, satin, fancy satin crepe.*

"I am a fabric designer for large French fabric companies. I also produce silk paintings for various uses such as wall hangings, paintings and accessories such as ties and shawls. Silk painting allows me to translate the images and impressions I capture in my mind during my travels and various situations. As far as the colors are concerned, I can obtain an infinite number of colors and shades. I am fascinated by color and mixing and this is what leads me to interpret these subtleties of color into my designs."

— Florence Niasse, Paris, France

### FLEUR DE POMMIER BLOUSE

Combined with the raglan jacket below, these make a complete outfit.

"I have worked for several well-known designers producing collections. I find silk painting "voluptuous." Its colors are so intense because of the brilliance of the silk. I personally enjoy drawing interlaced branches and "tortured" bark with scattered flowers. I feel that I actually produce paintings destined to enhance the female figure."
—Marie-Juliette Roux-Vigneron, Bourg-la-Reine, France

### RAGLAN JACKET

French dyes on silk with gutta serti; watercolor and alcohol techniques; hand quilted.
Marie-Juliette Roux-Vigneron

### ST. GEORGE AND THE DRAGON

French dyes and resist on
8mm China silk.
Len Brondum

### MORNING GLORIES

French dyes and resist on
8mm China silk.

"I have always been very interested in
the fine arts and painted in various other
mediums until I discovered silk painting.
I found that the vibrancy of the colors
and the beauty of the silk was the best
way to satisfy my creative abilities. I am
basically self-taught in silk painting,
using my art background, reading,
and experimenting. In addition to my
other subjects, I particularly enjoy
iconography."
— Len Brondum, New York

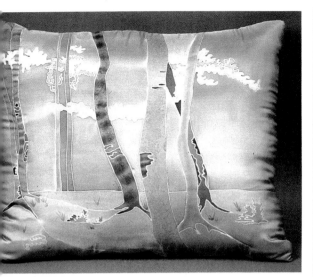

**LANDSCAPE**

*18" × 24"*

*Quilted silk cushion, French dyes and gutta resist.*

*"I am very taken with translating Oriental and whimsical themes into verbal designs on handpainted silk quilts. Movement in the designs is very important to me and is emphasized by the dimensional effect of quilting."*
— Ellen R. Backer, New York

**"SYNKU SYNKU"**

*82" × 43"*

*French dyes and gutta resist on silk. The title is taken from a Czechoslovakian folk song.*

*Ellen R. Backer*

## PORTRAIT OF MME. ZBOROWSKA

*Interpretation in silk of a painting by Modigliani*

*5mm silk, French dyes, antifusant technique.*

*Favart is an artist and teacher of silk painting.*

*Colette Favart-Gouin, Paris, France*

d'après Modigliani          C. favart

Portrait de Madame Zborowska

### SILK SCREENED AND HANDPAINTED YARDAGE

Complete design is painted in running yardage of 2.5 meters long, 90cm wide.

"First, just the black line was screen printed as a repeat pattern, using French colors with the appropriate thickener. It was steam set before the rest of the design was painted. This combination of techniques gave us a fine even line, which was used as the basis for the rest of the design, painted in "layers" (steamed between applications of color) to avoid the typical outlined look of resist. Some darker tones were painted directly over the lighter colors before steaming. The method we use takes a great deal of planning and painstaking application of dyes, but the unusual results are, in our opinion, worthwhile. This fabric found its way into a costume for a Dutch performer."

— Lee and Sheila Stewart, New York

**PERSIMMON ON A BRANCH**
*36" × 36"*
*5mm silk, dyes, gutta.*

*"I was visiting a friend in North Carolina and she showed me her favorite tree on her land — a very old persimmon tree covered with peach-colored fruit. It was fall and the tree's leaves had turned brown and lemon yellow. It was beautiful. I wanted to paint a branch of this tree on a silk scarf for my friend. As I completed my painting, I accidentally dripped a spot of orange dye onto my "perfect" background! What to do? Repeat the orange spots here and there to make the first one feel at home!"*
*— Jan Janas*

In writing this book, we have given you many suggestions to ensure a successful silk painting experience. We thought it would also be helpful to have a section where you could quickly look up the most common problems in silk painting with suggested solutions for correcting these problems. We hope you may never encounter these problems, but it's nice to know how to prevent or correct them if you do. As in most things, prevention is easier than correction. The suggestions may not work every time, but they're worth trying, particularly if you feel very unhappy with a silk painting.

As in all new endeavors, your first project may be far from perfect. But don't get discouraged. Success will come with practice! Silk painting is something to experience and *do*! It's not a mechanical art form. You're painting one-of-a-kind art pieces and no two are ever alike, so perfection is not the goal.

## *Problems Involving Resists*

**PROBLEM:** *The dyes flow outside the resist lines.*

**SOLUTION:** The fabric was not stretched tautly enough and had too much give when the resist was applied. This leads to an uneven application. Gaps are created, however minute. Wherever the resist has not completely surrounded even a single fiber, the color will flow through. In working with resists, consistently stretch your fabrics taut.

Or perhaps the opening in the resist applicator is too fine for the weight of the fabric used. In that case, change the size of the metal tip on the applicator. Or make a larger opening in the squeeze bottle if you are using one. When using a paper cone, if the hole is too small, enlarge it with a razor blade or needle or make another cone.

**PROBLEM:** *The consistency of the gutta is not correct for the weight of the fabric.*

**SOLUTION:** Add gutta solvent if it needs to be thinner. If it is too thin, keep it uncovered for a little while to let some solvent evaporate.

**PROBLEM:** *Air bubbles are creating gaps in the resist.*

**SOLUTION:** Let the resist rest in the applicator for a half hour so the air bubbles rise to the surface.

**PROBLEM:** *The line of resist is consistently too thin.*

**SOLUTION:** Move the applicator more slowly on the silk and push down sufficiently to let the resist penetrate.

**PROBLEM:** *The resist lines are too wide.*

**SOLUTION:** This happens when the resist is flowing too quickly out of the applicator. Change the size of the tip or make a new paper cone. Refrigerate the resist longer and apply it faster.

**PROBLEM:** *The blobs at the start and at the end of the resist lines are too prominent.*

**SOLUTION:** To minimize the blob at the start of a line, wipe the resist applicator tip with a paper towel before moving onto the fabric. To save time, put the paper on the fabric next to where you plan to begin, start your line on the paper, then move directly onto the fabric. When approaching the end of a line, gradually release the pressure on the applicator to decrease the size of the blob at the end.

**PROBLEM:** *You have accidentally dropped spots of resist on your fabric.*

**SOLUTION:**

• Don't hold your resist over the fabric. Keep your applicator resting on a paper towel in your other hand.

• Duplicate the spots and incorporate them in the overall design or add other shapes to change the design to hide them.

• If you're using water-soluble resist, rinse out the entire piece of fabric and start all over again.

• If you're using gutta, place a piece of folded cotton fabric (or cotton) under the spot. Use gutta solvent with a cotton swab. Rub the area and keep rubbing until the spot dissolves. Some of the gutta will remain in the fabric and that area will not take the colors in the same way. You can also dry-clean the entire piece to salvage it. Keep in mind that both resists, once removed, will give a very slight cast to the fabric and you might see some unevenness when you reuse the fabric. That can look quite interesting as it casts a random shadow. We personally find that very attractive.

**PROBLEM:** *After trying all the above suggestions, you may still have problems with resist application.*

**CAUSES:**

• You have too much or too little resist in your applicator or paper cone and that makes it hard to press evenly.

- On very heavy fabrics, you may need to apply the resist on both sides to coat the fibers completely. Weather conditions also affect resists: when it's very hot or humid, resists are difficult to control.
- You may have purchased a bad batch of resist or just have trouble with a particular brand. Try switching to a different brand or a different type of resist. And remember, gutta has a limited shelf life beyond which it won't be effective.
- Hasten the drying of resists with a hair dryer, but be very cautious. If the hair dryer is too close to the fabric, the water-soluble resist will disintegrate and gutta will dry too quickly and stop penetrating the fabric.

**PROBLEM: *A color has breached the resist.***
**SOLUTION:** There are several reasons why this might have happened:
- The problem may lie in the application of liquid color. We cannot emphasize strongly enough the care you must take in applying color to fabric within a resisted area. Always start from the center. Use the brush to stroke or guide the colors toward the line of resist and don't flood the area.
- If too much moisture is concentrated in one area, liquid will break through the line of resist. To correct this situation, "close the window." Just as the color flowed out in one direction, it will also move in the other when you paint the opposite area. Let the work dry completely before using the resist to close the gap. Then allow the resist to dry. Your resist will be colored at this point.
- If you're using traditional silk painting dyes, use alcohol and a cotton swab to quickly and carefully rub the stained area and decrease the intensity of the color. Paint the entire area where you've made the correction with special care. You can shade the area to hide it or use salt or alcohol to disguise it. Dotting that area by dry-brushing another color into it is also effective.
- If you are using resin-based silk paints, remove the color with soap and water and a cotton swab before it dries. Rub insistently.
- To avoid flooding an encircled area, practice loading the brush in the proper manner. Use a folded paper towel to consistently stroke off the excess color and work quickly.

Whatever happens, don't despair. Soon you will develop a feel for the quantity of liquid needed on the brush in relationship to the size of the area you're painting. Remember, the size of the brush must relate to the size of the surface you're

covering. Too small a brush will require too frequent dipping. Since the colors dry quickly, that might cause the rapid formation of dark edge lines with an uneven look. Too large a brush will tend to be overloaded. Always proceed with a light touch and a correctly loaded brush to cover a specific area.

**PROBLEM: *You have accidentally scattered salt in an unwanted area.***
**SOLUTION:** At this point, you may want to just add more salt to even out the design. You can use the larger salt effect as the start of a shape and use the pen technique to add interesting details to your design. You can also quickly repaint an entire area and use salt all over it again to give it a more even look.

If you prefer greater control over your use of salt, always wait for the areas that are not to be salted to dry completely before applying salt to other areas.

## Problems with Repainting
**PROBLEM: *Liquid was dropped on a silk painted surface before it was steam set.***
**SOLUTION:** Try duplicating the problem or incorporate it creatively into the design. Don't leave any liquids (coffee, water or paint) near a silk painting. Always clean off any liquid color from the frame before you remove the silk. (A wet brush is also a threat!) As soon as a silk painting is dry, roll it up for steaming and place it in a plastic bag to protect it. If you live in a humid area, do not use a plastic bag—condensation may form inside it. Use a paper bag instead.

**PROBLEM: *You must repaint an entire area because it is not pleasing.***
**SOLUTION:**
- If the color is wrong, use a darker color and swiftly go over the entire area to avoid the formation of the dark edge line. But be careful. As long as the color is not set, the colors can change. For instance, placing blue over yellow will give you a green.
- If the area is uneven, swiftly repaint the entire area using a stiff brush and scrub the areas where you wish to remove some of the dark edge lines. Try to push the color toward the line of resist—it will migrate and form a lovely ring there. This is effective with the traditional silk painting dyes only. After being subjected to resin-based colors, the fabric loses some of its hand when repainted.

**PROBLEM:** *You have completely finished a project and the colors are wrong—too loud, too dark, too light, etc.*

**SOLUTION:** *If the fabric has not been steam set,* you can reapply resist, add shapes, and repaint certain areas to change the look. Repainting will make the resist lines the color of the background, which is very attractive. Certain select areas can be repainted, details added, and the entire surface repainted with a wash. The wash will probably cause a lot of streaking, which can be quite beautiful.

Perhaps the colors are too loud or you simply don't like them and are willing to try more drastic solutions. In that case, prepare a dye bath with a tint or light color—or use just plain water or an alcohol solution, if you want less extreme results. Quickly dip the entire fabric in the solution, open it up carefully, and hang it to dry without allowing the surfaces to overlap. Again, this method is not effective with resin-based paints.

When using traditional silk painting dyes, you can also remove all the color from painted fabrics before they are steam set. First rinse the fabric in hot water to remove as much dye as possible. Mix one capful of ammonia-based all-purpose cleaner in a pot of water, add the silk, bring to a boil, and simmer for approximately seven minutes. Rinse the silk. This hot rinse can also be done in the microwave. Use a microwave-safe dish and heat seven minutes. All the dye should disappear.

*If the fabric has already been steam set,* you are essentially working over colored fabric. In that case, you can apply resist again and repaint certain areas or apply a wash with a wide brush over the entire surface.

## Accidents in Steam Setting

**PROBLEM:** *You have just had an accident while steam setting your fabric.*

**SOLUTION:** Take an honest look at the effects. They may be quite unusual. You may be able to think of the result as a special work of art. Or, if you can't save the entire painting, you may be able to select certain areas of the fabric and use it for covering a box, decorating a card, or making jewelry. You can also cover small areas with quilting or appliqués to hide problems.

Textiles are used for domestic purposes on a daily basis, as well as for festive occasions and in places of worship. They are a symbol of social and economic status. We feel that painted silks and fabrics have finally taken their place among prized fabrics in our society. They are aesthetically pleasing and functional.

Here is a list of the many uses for your silk paintings. Always sign your silk art. It is one of a kind and will become valuable!

**FOR ARTISTIC DISPLAY.** Framed artwork—wall hangings—wearable art to display—banners—miniature framed silk paintings.

**FOR INTERIOR DESIGN.** Pillows—drapes—shades—bedspreads—tablecloths, napkins—place mats—lamp shades—fabric to drape ceilings and walls—screens—room dividers.

**QUILTED SILK PAINTING.** Quilted bedspread—quilted wall hangings—padded and/or quilted walls for total environment—quilted wearable art.

**WEARABLE ART.** Dresses—blouses—skirts—vests—shirts—jackets—coordinated sets—coats—suits—lingerie—cotton shirts and sets for casual wear—scarves, plain and tube—shawls—wedding dresses—linings for handwoven garments—all items for men and women.

**FASHION ACCESSORIES.** Ties—bow ties—cummerbunds—jewelry—evening bags—handkerchiefs—canvas bags—painted lace.

**RITUAL OBJECTS.** Vestments—altar covers—wall decorations—wedding canopies—ark curtains—tallisim—challah covers—head covers.

**MISCELLANEOUS.** Silk flowers—kites—covered boxes—covered books—basket liners—as a vehicle to reproduce fabrics and prints on fabric or paper.

## Framing and Hanging Painted Silk

After working so hard to create beautiful paintings, don't fail to share them with others. The many ways to complete and frame your work is beyond the scope of this book (we'll reserve that for a future project which will include how to engineer and design silk painted wearable art). But here are a few suggestions to help you preserve and enjoy your work:

When hanging your art, place it away from direct sunlight and heat vents. Occasionally dust it. It is preferable to frame the art under glass but without the glass touching the silk. To hang your silk paintings as a banner, sew a pocket at the top and insert a firm rod. Do the same at the bottom so that you will have a smooth surface or, if you prefer the silk to move, allow the bottom to hang free.

We hope that you will enjoy using and living with your artwork as well as selling and giving it to others.

## Bibliography

Avon-Coffrant, Francoise. *Manuel Pratique de la Peinture sur Soie*. Paris: Arted, 1987.

Bain, Litza. *Magie et Technique de la Peinture sur Soie*. Cahier Nos. 1 et 2. Paris: Published by Litza Bain, 1978.

Bain, Litza. *Guide de la Peinture sur Soie*. Paris: Dessain et Tolra, 1987.

Kolander, Cheryl. *A Silk Worker's Notebook*. Myrtle Creek, Oregon: Published by Cheryl Kolander, 1979.

Lavenant, Daniel. *Peindre sur Soie*. Paris: Dessain et Tolra, 1978.

Libessart, Regine. *Le Livre Complet de la Peinture sur Soie*. Paris: Editions Fleurus, 1987.

Mendes, Valerie D. and Hinchcliffe, Frances M., *Ascher*. London: Victoria and Albert Museum. 1987.

Ottelart, Lydie. *Nouvelle Techniques pour la Peinture sur Soie*. Paris: Dessain et Tolra, 1986.

Ottelart, Lydie. *L'Aquarelle sur Soie*. Paris: Dessain et Tolra, 1988.

Tuckman, Diane and Barsky, Naomi. *The New Grapevine: A Silk Painting Guide*. Beltsville, MD: Published by Ivy Imports, 1989.

# PERMISSIONS

## Artist Credits

We would like to thank the following artists for permitting us to use their works in this volume. (Those works that are untitled are noted by a descriptive phrase.)

**Alison Abbott** and **Lynn Weinberg**, *Silkscapes: Faces* Scarf, p. 33; *Silkscapes: Gauguin,* Scarf and Purse, p. 102.

**Sharon M. Adee**, Scarf and Earrings, p. 5; *Fragmentary Alliance*—Jacket, and Scarf, p. 101.

**Ellen R. Backer**, *Synku Synku* and *Landscape*, p. 113. Original design and execution by Ellen R. Backer.

**Litza Bain**, *Barreaux de Sel*, p. 92.

**Dominique Bello**, Cocoon Jacket, p. 21; Geometric Wall Hanging, p. 94.

**Sharon A. Blake**, *Jazz*, p. 89. An adaptation of a Henri Matisse illustration from the book (*Jazz*).

**Andree Borremans**, *Butterflies*, *Bird*, and *Orchids*, pp. 106, 107.

**Len Brondum**, *St. George and the Dragon* and *Morning Glories*, p. 112. Paintings on silk by Len Brondum of Canandaigua, NY.

**Constance Byrd**, Scarves, p. 92.

**Jennifer Cauffman** of Glory Fibers, *Whale Watch*, p. 98.

**Devereaux Chivington**, *Hanged Man*, p. 85. © 1989 by Devereaux Chivington; loaned from the Eric Stanton collection.

**Mme. Florence Denise Corpron**, *Floral*, p. 74.

**Earllene Dakan-Weiss**, Tunic Top and Wall Hanging, p. 103.

**Colette Favart-Gouin**, *Interpretation in silk of a painting by Modigliani (Portrait of Mme. Zborowska)*, p. 114.

**W. Logan Fry**, *Piscine Transformation* and *Carrot-Top Meets the Annelid*, p. 104.

**Hilary Gifford**, Fabric Detail and Wall Hanging, pp. 86, 87.

**Alison Gray**, *Boats at Menemsha* and *Winter Logs*, p. 99.

**Joan Griffin**, *Impression of a Butterfly*, p. 4. © 1989, Joan Griffin.

**Terri Higgs**, Yardage for Kimono, p. 45.

**Jane B. Ihndris**, *Framed Landscape*, p. 41; *Landscape*, p. 63. Original design and painting by Jane B. Ihndris.

**Marie-Laure Ilie**, *Apparition*, p. 82. © Marie-Laure Ilie.

**Joni Johns**, Kimono, p. 95.

**Mary Klotz**, *Shibori Scarf Variation*, p. 100. © 1989, Mary T. Klotz, Frederick, MD

**Anne-Lan**, *Lilith*, p. 108. © Anne-Lan, Paris, France.

**Claudia MacGruer**, Man's Shirt, p. 94.

**Maria Malmberg**, *Summer Roses*, p. 105.

**Phyllis McLean**, Jacket, p. 102.

**Pennie Miller**, Silk Scarves, pp. 25, 26, 35.

**Florence Niasse**, *Personnages Naif* and *Design and Puzzle* (dresses), p. 110.

**Linda A. Prenger**, *Vase of Flowers*, p. 97. © 1988, Linda S. Prenger.

**Carol Racklin-Siegel**, *Aztec Birds, Landscape Tryptic, Japanese Landscape Tryptic*, p. 93. © 1989, Carol Racklin-Siegel.

**Betty Ricketts**, Pre-constructed Colored Shirt, p. 78.

**Leslie Rogers**, *Tide Waning* and *Garden Flowers*, p. 84.

**Marie-Juliette Roux-Vigneron** "Norengiu," Fleur de Pommier (Raglan Jacket), Blouse and Skirt, p. 111.

**Sandra Rubel**, Pleated Ensemble and Gossamer Gown and Shawl, p. 90.

**Jan Ryan**, *La Danseuse aux Serpents*, p. 88.

**Lee and Sheila Stewart**, Handpainted Fabric, p. 115.

**Shar Tikkanen**, *Ricky Henderson*, p. 96. Permission of National Baseball Library, Cooperstown, NY

**Christa VanValkenburg**, Silk Patchwork Jacket, p. 95.

**Shirley T. Waxman**, *Family Tree* and *Challah Cover*, p. 109.

**Angela Marie Woodruff**, *Venus Comb Murex Seashell*, p. 91. An original design and painting by Angela Marie Woodruff.

## Photographer Credits

All photographs by Robert Leonard unless otherwise noted below:

**Susan Abrams**, *La Danseuse aux Serpents* (by Jan Ryan), p. 88.

**Janice Felgar**, Tunic Top and Wall Hanging (by Earllene Dakan-Weiss), p. 103. Photo © Janice Felgar.

**Steve Green**, *Whale Watch* (by Jennifer Cauffman of Glory Fibers), p. 98.

**Bob Hanson**, *Landscape* (by Ellen Backer), p. 113.

**Jan Janas**, Yardage for Kimono (by Terri Higgs), p. 45; also pp. 2, 5, 6 (bottom), 8, 22 (top), 33, 39 (top), 40 (left), 43, 44, 49 (bottom), 65, 71, 116.

**Richard S. Lerner**, Kimono (by Joni Johns), p. 95.

**Doug Long**, *Synku Synku* (by Ellen Backer), p. 113.

**Red Elf**, *Vase of Flowers* (by Linda Prenger), p. 97.

**Paul Rocheleau**, Man's Shirt (by Claudia MacGruer), p. 94.

**Jean Schnell**, *Piscine Transformation* and *Carrot-Top Meets the Annelid* (by W. Logan Fry), p. 104.

**Gary Sinick**, *Aztec Birds, Landscape Tryptic*, and *Japanese Landscape Tryptic* (by Carol Racklin-Siegel), p. 93.

**Harriet Wise**, *Shibori Scarf Variation* (by Mary Klotz), p. 100.

# INDEX